It Had to Happen

Memoirs From an Abused Child

Book One

Mattie Williams

Copyright © 2022 by Mattie Williams

All rights reserved. No part of this book may be reproduced or transmitted in any form or by any means without written permission from the author.

Hardback ISBN 979-8-9865863-0-4

Ebook ISBN 979-8-9865863-1-1

Printed in USA by 48HrBooks (www.48HrBooks.com)

First Edition

Edited by Ebonique Little

Book design by Brittnee Smith Creative Co.

Photograph on back cover: Photography by Bob Thomas

Dedication

This book is dedicated to my wonderful husband, Gerald Williams Jr.; my two beautiful children, Kyra and Kayden; and my dear mother and sisters. I love you all!!

It Had to Happen is dedicated to all of the children who endured physical, mental, sexual, and/or emotional abuse from their loved ones. To the children who suffer in silence because the expectation is to pretend everything is going well, I want you to know that you can speak up and advocate for yourself in order to get the help you need. *It Had to Happen* is for adults who grew up with unresolved trauma and are trying to live life and be successful. My story is for you to see that you are not alone, that you can overcome your trauma and become prosperous.

Foreword

This book is a compilation of unfiltered, unedited moments in the life of the writer who has always been transparent and honest. She understands that every event and every moment in her life has led her to this point in time; although some of the moments may be saddening, all events were lessons that paved the writer's journey and ushered her safely into adulthood.

I've been graced to have known Mattie for more than two decades, and am extremely proud to call her my niece and friend. She is dear to my heart! I've watched her persevere through obstacles that would have destroyed, or at least deterred, many; yet Mattie, through tears, suffering, and hardships, has never let her greatest light of love and laughter grow dim.

She has always been passionate, strong-willed, forthright, and resilient. Her tenacity is unmatched! She is a phenomenal

God-fearing wife to a wonderful husband and a sweet mother who rears her children intentionally to be thankful for all things and respectful of all people.

As you scroll through each page of this memoir, please remember that people are flawed and in need of a Savior. Most importantly, that grace wins every time!

Lovingly,

Aunt Tinkle

Table of Contents

Foreword — iv

Introduction: Message from the Author-The Dream — 1

Chapter 1: The Lost Voice — 9

Chapter 2: Finding My Voice — 15

Chapter 3: My Mother's Struggle — 20

Chapter 4: North Filthadelphia — 32

Chapter 5: A Product of my Enviornment — 40

Chapter 6: The Block — 48

Chapter 7: The Mystery House — 59

Chapter 8: The Good Times — 68

Chapter 9: Daddy Issues — 84

Chapter 10: Lyfe — 94

Chapter 11: Caught — 112

Chapter 12: The Red Carpet — 121

Chapter 13: School — 126

Chapter 14: The Privileged Girl — 145

Chapter 15: The New School — 158

Chapter 16: Revenge — 165

Chapter 17: China Plates   171

Chapter 18: The Prayer   179

Chapter 19: The Last Straw   181

Chapter 20: The Great Separation   198

The Dream

I have been trying to write this book for 10 years and was unsuccessful because of fear and doubt. Actually, I could have had this book finished when I first decided I wanted to write a book way back in 2011, but the fear of writing about my life took me back to the time my journals were used against me in the court of law. I had so much material in my journals, which would have made it so much easier for me to write this book, but they were taken away from me in court as evidence and were never returned. From the ages of 12 to 16, I wrote in a journal daily, writing things that were going on in my life. You know, the normal teenaged journaling like, *I hate it here, I want to run away, and I hate my life*, along with other traumatic experiences I have endured. My journals were taken when I was 16 in court testifying against my rapist, which will be revealed in Book Two. This discouraged me from writing in a diary or writing anything personal from 2011 up until 2019. Once I mustered up the courage to start writing again and got over the fear of my writings being used to expose my flaws, I had a dream.

The morning of January 15, 2019, I had a dream that I was at a pool with my family, my husband and my two children, during a family vacation. There were a few gentlemen dressed in all black suits who came to the pool to recruit young ladies and adult women to work for them in the streets. The job description was to sell your body for money, dance on poles for money, and sell drugs for money. *They must not have had an updated picture of my child bearing body, because it ain't cute*. These gentlemen had top secret information on the young ladies they were looking for in the folders they carried. Each young lady had a folder with their name on it, with information about their past inside the folder. The gentleman who came to me said that I meet the qualifications based on my background because I was a physically and sexually abused foster child. To me, this meant that I must think low of myself, or that I am damaged. Even though I am grown and have my own family now, I still wasn't worth being happy or having my own prosperous life. It was as if, because I went through those things, I was destined to be damaged goods like no one would want me, that maybe I was incapable to love and be loved. At 5:45 a.m., I woke up just in time for my morning prayer with my aunt. I explained to her how the dream had discouraged me a little bit, and brought back to my memory those horrible things I went through as a child. Now, I know it was just a dream, but the enemy will find ways to get into your head to discourage you and make you feel like you're not worth anything. I encourage you not to give up on yourself, on your family, on your life and dreams, just because you endured serious trauma in your life. Although it was a dream, to be honest, I started to feel some type of way. I started to feel self-doubt. I started to wonder if my husband really loved me or if I was part of some charity give away. I started to wonder if I was a good enough parent to my children. Deep down inside, I know I am a good wife and mother, but this dream really did have me thinking about my self-worth.

Honestly, I have to let you know that I am not the most spiritual person, and I won't be preaching throughout this book, but I know the enemy to be a liar. I know that he comes to kill, steal, and destroy me and my family (John 10:10 paraphrased). I prayed through it, and I declared out of my mouth that my past trauma doesn't depict how I am as an adult. I prayed that if I am in Christ, my past is dead; now, I am a new person (2 Corinthians 5:17). Sometimes things will show up in life that will remind you of your past and try to knock you off your mark, but you have to pray through them and remind yourself that God has brought you out of those situations for a reason, which may be so that you can be of some encouragement to someone else. Not only was I reminded of what happened to me in my past during a dream, but I was reminded yesterday at work from a seventh grader, who shared with me that she was physically abused by her mother before. I let her vent to me about her previous issues with her mother, and how she felt like she was alone and different from everyone else because she was in a foster home. I calmly told her it is okay to be different, that not everyone lives with their mother or father. What I didn't share with her, was that I went through a similar situation. I was caught up on teaching and doing my job, that I couldn't see a child needed my story to encourage her and make her feel better. I should have told her that I was physically abused by my mother and that I became a foster child, as well. That is the one thing I regret, not taking the time to share.

My purpose in life is to share what I know with young women and men. I want them to know there are answers and options and that they can persevere. I want to encourage them to push past their traumatic experiences and make something of themselves. During the very traumatic experiences in my life, I felt alone. I didn't try to reach out for help until it was too late, when the damage had been done. I didn't think anyone cared for me enough to want to help me, so I didn't bother to ask. Most ignorantly, I thought I was the only person going through these traumatic experiences. I thought that if I shared what was really going on in my life, I would be judged and looked down upon. If you are a young person or adult reading this book, I want to let you know that you are not alone, that you are not the only person who suffered through those experiences, nor will you be the only person to go through this, and get out of it successfully. I encourage you to get help by talking to someone who you can confide in, someone that can help see you out of your circumstance. I pray you will rise above your past and encourage other young ladies and gentlemen to rise, as well. I hope this book will encourage you to rise. I pray the stories of my life will encourage someone to live out their best life, no matter what they went through, no matter what they are going through, and no matter how many things or people try to remind you of all the horrible things that have happened to you. You can rise above it and move on to be a great and successful person. This dream I had was meant to stop me from writing; instead, it pushed me to write more and get my story out so that it could reach you. This dream was meant to set me back and make me doubt myself, make me doubt my life. Instead, it helped me look at my life differently and understand why I went through what I did. The only thing that came to mind was "It Had to Happen!" If I had not gone through this trauma, I would have never known strength the way I do now. I would not know that I could endure and push past my trauma, and turn it into something beautiful and powerful. I would not have fought so hard to change the narrative of my life from stuck to stable and established. This dream woke me up, honey; it encouraged me to write, to pray, and live my best life, knowing that God has never left me, nor will He forsake me.

Knowing that God had brought me out of all that mess, has renewed my strength, my mind, body and soul. I always wanted to write a book; I was always a writer. I stopped because I let my past get the best of me. Reliving my past was hard; it started to bring old traumatic experiences to my new life. It started to make me a bitter and angry person. I started to treat my immediate family differently because I was falling back into the abyss of hurt, shame, and abuse. I wasn't ready at that time, but God placed it on my heart to try again, and here I am, an author, following my dreams. I am finally at a place where I can share my story through word of mouth and words on a page to help encourage young ladies and gentlemen that they can make it through life. Never give up, never lose sight of what you want to accomplish; instead, push through and be the change this world needs. Everything that you are going to read in this book Had to Happen, so that you can read this book and be encouraged to keep pushing, and make something of your life.

The Lost Voice

Growing up in a house that was quiet, but loud in so many ways, was how I discovered my lost voice. There was the noise from outside on the block; I could hear the kids on the block running, laughing, and having fun. There was the noise from my mother speaking on the phone or her yelling at my sisters and me inside the house. It was sometimes quiet in my mind, but mostly loud, because I had so many thoughts about what I wanted to say, but couldn't say and what I wanted to do, but couldn't do. I had no platform to speak in my house. I couldn't speak up for myself, as my voice was lost in fear, neglect, and physical abuse. My mother used famous lines like, "you're a child, stay in a child's place" and "children should be seen, and not heard." There were so many other mantras she used, like "shut the fuck up" and "stop all that god damned noise," followed by threats and physical abuse. Whenever I was given the chance to speak, my voice shook in fear of what would come as a result of my speaking. I was smacked across my face, and my life was threatened on many different occasions, for simply answering questions asked of me. This didn't necessarily give me the courage I needed to speak up to my mother, or anyone else, for that matter. That same fear followed me throughout my childhood and most of my adult life. As a result, I am a soft-spoken person. Oftentimes when asked to speak at school or anywhere else, I would be asked to speak louder so that I could be heard. Deep inside, I felt it didn't matter how loud I spoke. I would still never be heard because my voice was lost, and to me, it didn't matter. For without a voice, I could never be heard.

Going to school with a lost voice wasn't easy. People picked on me because I was "different." I was the dirty girl whose parents sent her to school with the signs of neglect and physical abuse. Unkept, I entered school daily with dirty second-hand clothes, with my hair standing on the top of my head. I went to school with open welts, colored bruises, and busted lips. I was the quiet one in the class who didn't talk to others or participate in class discussions without being forced to do so by my teachers. I couldn't find my voice to speak up for myself, so I let people walk all over me. I let them tease me because if I did say something, I would get into a fight at school, and then I would have to get in a fight at home with my mother. Don't get me twisted, I can hold my own. I did get into some fights, (actually, lots of fights because of my sister) but if it were up to me, I wouldn't fight because I was already in the fight of my life at home every night. *Now that I think about it, even me fighting for and with my sister was an act of the lost voice I had discovered.* I couldn't even tell her I didn't want to fight. Even though I knew she knew my feelings, I didn't matter, so I didn't even bother to speak up. At that time, I wasn't ready to find my voice just yet, so I continued to let people hit, tease, and taunt me every day. Sometimes, I wished I was like my other two sisters, Lyfe and Phoenix (Fifi). They didn't have a voice at home, either, so they shouted at school. Lyfe and Fifi were always in trouble, always fighting and winning those fights at school, but when they got home, boy, did they have a new and tougher fight with my mom they never won. My mother was very strict; she taught me to respect my elders, and be good at school so I didn't get in trouble. If I disobeyed any of those rules — or sometimes, just simply breathed or existed around my mother — it would be doomsday. But somehow, trouble always found me, the dirty kid.

The voice inside of me wanted so badly to be heard. I was angry; I wanted to fight back at school; I wanted to fight my mother, but I knew that wouldn't pan out well. Under normal circumstances when a child gets froggy and leaps at their parents, they might get a smack to the face or a good cussing out, but in my house, I would get a hand to the neck until my feet were dangling from the floor as I squirmed, gasping for air. I would get a two-by-four upside my head or a beating butt naked with an extension cord straight out the bath.

I'm reminded of the time when my mother came home late at night (more like early morning), drunk from a speakeasy. She came through the front door and straight across to the bottom of the steps, fussing about how the house wasn't clean. "I told y'all bitches to clean my damn house before I got back home, and it's not clean," my mom yelled in a sluggish voice as she started to approach the steps. My sisters and I were upstairs in our rooms asleep when we heard her voice. We came running out of our rooms to the top of the stairs where my mother met us. "Mommy, we cleaned the house for you just like you asked," I responded in a calm and sleepy, childlike voice.

Well, my mother didn't like that because I spoke out of turn. "Did I ask you to say anything?" my mother said, doinking (poking) her finger on my forehead.

"No ma'am," I replied, putting my head down looking at the floor. Being careful not to look my mother in the eyes, because that would be like I'm challenging her, which would not be good. She then smacked me in my face and grabbed my neck with one hand choking me, lifting me from the floor.

"If you ever disrespect me again, I will kill yo' ass," my mother said. I was crying, as my sisters stood there crying, as well.

"Ye-s m-am," I muttered through the sharp pain in my neck. My mother took and threw me down 14 steps, from the very top step to the very bottom step. The first impact was when I hit about the sixth step from the top, and then rolled and flipped down the rest of the stairs. That day, I believed I broke my ankle, but I couldn't even express my pain in such a way that would accuse my mother of breaking my bones. I cried, and limped, and cried some more. "Shut that damn noise up!" my mother yelled. Through my fear, I suppressed my pain and told myself to suck it up as I cried silent tears. I had a limp for weeks. "What the hell is wrong with you walking around here like that?" my mother would ask me. I would just make up some random story of how I fell at school or something. I was afraid to tell her the truth. I had to find a way that would not seem challenging. How could I say, "I am limping because YOU threw me down the steps," without it sounding like an accusation? *Even though it wouldn't be an accusation because it is the true fact that she literally threw me down the stairs,* but she wouldn't have seen it that way. I could see her whipping my behind again. As a result, I kept my voice down inside myself, and chose to keep my lost voice because finding my voice at home normally wasn't a good idea.

Finding My Voice

There were times when I thought I'd found my voice, like the time my mother fell on ice and broke both of her legs. My mom fell after the "Blizzard of '96." She couldn't get around much, so I thought this would be a great time to find my voice. *She can't move; she won't be able to hurt me,* I thought. One day I was acting up at school, (when I say I was acting up, it means I was really just sticking up for myself, going back and forth with the usual bullies who bothered me). Before today I was afraid to stick up for myself because I was terrified to get in trouble at home with my mother, not because I was afraid of the kids. My teacher said, "Tameena, I'm going to have to have a talk with your mother." Now under normal circumstances, I would be like, "Oh no, I'm sorry. Please don't call my mother." In fact, my teacher wouldn't even need to say anything to me because I kept quiet. However, this day, *oh, this day*, I found my voice! I told my teacher, "I don't care. She won't answer because her legs are broke and she still in the hospital!" I didn't even think twice about saying it; it just came out. I FOUND MY VOICE! When I got home, my mother was home from the hospital, sitting on the long cream couch with the plastic on it, with casts on both legs and a pair of crutches. All of the sudden, I lost my voice again. *Well, that was short lived. I became hoarse as my voice left me swiftly.* The fear my mother put in me all came back in one swoop before she could even open her mouth.

"So, you think that just because I hurt myself, you can go to school and act a fool?

"No ma'am," I replied with the words barely escaping my mouth.

"GET yo' ass over here," my mother said in a decrescendo voice, but with a tight lip.

Nothing but fear flashed through my mind. Now you would think, that I would think, that because my mother couldn't get around, I would continue to have a voice and be tough like I was at school. Nope, not me. My scary, no-voice-having self, went right over to her as she ordered and took the beat down with a crutch. *Yup, you read it; she beat me with a crutch.* I walked over to where she was sitting and was kind of standing over her. My mother punched me in my stomach, grabbed me by the back of the neck pulling me down to her level, and punched and smacked my head. As she was hitting me, I fell lower to the floor and felt the crutch knocking me on my head and body. I was crying and squirming all around the floor next to her as the beating ended. "The next time you want to be smart and talk back to your teachers, yo' ass is mine. Don't think because my legs are broke, I still can't whip yo' ass," my mother said, out of breath. I had no voice and no feeling in my body after that beating.

In the midst of all that was happening in my home life, I thought I found my voice through singing. I would listen to different types of music that moved me. I learned that I could carry a note, so I started singing songs (in my head). I guess you could call it silent singing. I started writing music and poems in my notebook, which also became my diary. Unfortunately, in my house, I was not able to sing out loud. I didn't have the courage to open my mouth at home to speak, so I was most definitely not going to open my mouth to sing at home, at least not unless I was ordered to sing. There were times my mom would listen to her oldies when she got drunk. She got drunk very often; so much that at the age of nine, I knew just about every oldie there was. Sometimes if my mother wasn't too drunk, she would sing oldies as she cooked. Oh, and my mother could cook. On Thanksgiving, my mother would make a big spread. There would be macaroni and cheese, turkey, ham, collard greens, string beans, candied yams, potato salad, stuffing, cranberry sauce, and so much more. Her food was delicious, but when she wasn't home to cook (which was very often), I had to fend for myself. I just wished she had cooked more, but I digress, *focus on singing*. My mother would have my sisters and I come and sing with her. It would be early in the morning or late at night, and she would get us out of bed to sing with her when she was drunk. It didn't matter the time to me; it was a time my mom was in an okay mood, and it was something I loved to do. It was a chance for me to show her that I could sing, that I liked singing, but her drunkenness wouldn't allow her to notice my talent. I thought my voice was going to be found then, but it was lost in the drunkenness of my mother's spirit. This lost and found voice followed me along the rest of my life.

My Mother's Struggle

My mother was number seven out of 14 children, born in Richmond, Virginia in 1953. My grandmother dropped my mother off at her sister's house when she was around 11 months old. Aunt Jacky, who is my great aunt, took care of my mother while Grandmother worked for a white family. Aunt Jacky was nice, but strict and hard on my mother. She taught my mother how to respect her elders, how to be a good person, and introduced her to God and church. Although Aunt Jacky took care of my mother, she didn't stop her husband from sexually abusing my mother.

My mother only knew Aunt Jacky as her mother, because no one told her about the switcharoo that transpired when she was an infant. So, the strictness, and beatings were normal to my mother. Aunt Jacky's husband, my mother's "father" Uncle Melvin, was molesting and raping my mother from age 10 until 13. Uncle Melvin was a famous gospel singer who traveled all around the world. He went to sing about the Lord and then came home and raped my mother.

Uncle Melvin would snatch my mother out of her bed at night when his wife was working, and put my mother in his bed and have his way with her. One night while Uncle Melvin was raping my mother, Aunt Jacky came home from work and peeked in on them, opening the door slightly, but she didn't say anything; she closed the door and turned back around. My mother saw her peeking, but my mother never said a word. Aunt Jacky blamed my mother the next day by throwing Uncle Melvin's clothes at her to iron. "Since you want to be grown, iron his clothes for him," Aunt Jacky said to my mother with a snarky attitude. That's when the relationship changed for my mother and Aunt Jacky. Aunt Jacky started to treat my mother like Uncle Melvin's mistress. My mother prayed so many sleepless nights that her father wouldn't come into her room, but he came, anyway. He went into my mother's room, and while she was awake in fear, started grabbing her and pulling her away from the bed. My mother did everything she could to hold on to the corners of her bed; she kicked and screamed, but she wasn't strong enough. Uncle Melvin continued to rape her for years, until the day she overheard some ghastly news.

At age 13, my mother overheard her "mother and father" talking about my grandmother, my mother's real mother.

"So, when are you going to tell her?" her father Uncle Melvin said to his wife, Aunt Jacky.

Her mother Aunt Jacky responded, "Tell her what?"

"When are you going to tell her that we are not her real parents?" Uncle Melvin responded.

Aunt Jacky responded, "I guess we have to tell her today because her mother will be stopping by soon."

My mother continued to eavesdrop and was so heartbroken when she heard the news.

While my mother's parents planned how they were going to enter her room to tell her the news, my mother started putting two and two together. She always wondered why her dad would rape her, but now she knows that Uncle Melvin wasn't her dad. *Maybe this is why he was raping me, because he didn't care about me. He didn't love me like a father loves a child. Maybe that's why Aunt Jacky allowed it to happen because she didn't care about me, because I wasn't really her daughter,* my mother thought. Out of fear and anxiety about next steps, my mother just buried her head down into her knees and started to cry until Aunt Jacky and Uncle Melvin entered the room.

Aunt Jacky and Uncle Melvin entered my mother's bedroom to find her crying. They didn't know she overheard their conversation.

"What's wrong?" Aunt Jacky asked.

"I know that you are not my real parents," my mother said, sobbing.

"Oh, I am so sorry you had to find out this way," Aunt Jacky responded.

"We were going to tell you, but we could never find the right time," Uncle Melvin added.

They went on to tell my mother that her real mother was going to show up soon to take her.

"But I don't even know her; she just can't come and take me from you, can she?" my mother sobbed.

"Sadly yes, because there are no legal documents to say you can stay with me," Aunt Jacky replied.

Aunt Jacky didn't want my mother to go, but she left the decision up to my mother to choose. When my grandmother showed up, out of fear, my mother chose to go back with my grandmother. All types of thoughts ran through her head like, *If I don't go, she will be mad at me, or she will find me and steal me away from Aunt Jacky. I don't want to stay here either because Uncle Melvin rapes me.* She was too afraid to say no to her mother. *Perhaps my mother had a lost voice too, like me. It's something how fear will drag you into situations that you know are not good for you. Fear of the unknown itself can take over your brain, let alone fear of the known.* My mother didn't know my grandmother from a can of spray paint. *Why would she choose to go back with her after all these years?* I often ask myself. I guess my mother thought things couldn't get much worse; after all, she was being raped by her "father uncle" often. My mother was between a rock and a hard place, but she had to make a choice.

My grandmother helped my mother pack her things, and they left Virginia to travel to Chester, Pennsylvania, where my grandmother lived. Living in Chester was one of the worst places to live. The crime and drug rate were always high. My grandmother physically abused my mother for a year, until my mother decided to run away. One winter day, my grandmother gave my mother 35 cents to go to the store to buy a small container of bleach and White Cap Pine-Oil cleaner (my favorite cleaning chemical). She walked to the store with a scarf, pajamas, and bedroom slippers, but no coat or jacket to keep her warm. My mother thought she was just making a quick stop to the corner store and straight back home. As she walked to the store, she realized she didn't want to go back home. Instead of walking there, my mother went past the corner store and kept walking.

Not knowing where to go, my mother just walked the streets of Chester with 35 cents in her pocket. During the walk, men honked their horns at her as if she was a prostitute. My mother kept walking until she reached 69th Street. It started to snow, but she just kept walking in her slippers. White men pulled over to try to give her "a ride," but she declined. A white undercover cop tried to stop my mom. He thought she was a prostitute. He kept trying to solicit her services, so that he could arrest her, but my mother denied being a prostitute every time. Then, the undercover police officer announced that he was a police officer and asked her where she needed to go. My mother said she was trying to get to Delaware. The police officer took my mother to get something to eat, put his coat around her, and then gave her $50 to get on the bus to Delaware. All in all, my mother needed someone to love her, so she went looking for love in all the wrong places. From the age of 14, my mother was all on her own and did whatever she needed to survive. That's when the real struggle began.

Years later, I was born in North Philadelphia. I am the eighth of ten children. I lived in a poor neighborhood where poverty, violence, and drug abuse were always at an all-time high. Most of the houses were Section 8 houses for low-income families that couldn't afford nice housing. There was also a different affordable housing program called "the projects." There was project housing all around North Philadelphia, but no matter which one you lived in, it was called "the projects," especially when people would explain where they or someone else lived. I'm not sure how true this statement is, but it was said that the acronym for the projects was **P**eople **R**elying **O**n **J**ust **E**nough **I**ncome **T**o **S**urvive. The acronym seemed correct to me, considering one's rent would be determined their income. Depending on one's income a person could pay anywhere from $0-$200 a month at that time. The Philadelphia Housing Authorities (PHA) owned the projects and Section 8 houses and didn't feel the need to keep them up to date or renovate them at all. For people of color didn't need nice things if they couldn't afford to have nice things. The houses were old and run down or just simply not taken care of properly. Almost anything free in the hood came with a price of incompetence, negligence, and lack of human care.

I lived in the Raymond Rosen Projects when I was a baby until I was about four or five years old. Raymond Rosen spanned a few blocks, and there were small one or two-floor row homes and high risers. I lived on 23rd and Diamond Street in one of the approximately eight to 10 high rise buildings. The high rises were the taller buildings that had about 13 to 15 floors. Each floor serviced about 10 to 12 families, and my family was one out of the many. I don't remember much about living in the projects, except that we lived on one of the top floors. I used to look out the windows and think I lived in a castle of some sort. *Silly me to think I could live in a castle.*

My mother had 10 children, eight girls and two boys, by the time she was 30 years old. At the time we were living in the projects, there were only nine of us living with my mother; one of my sisters was in foster care since birth. My mother was a high school dropout because she got pregnant with my oldest sister Trina, and had to rely on the government to supply her with the basic needs of living. My mother tried to find work to help provide for her children, but without a high school diploma, it was almost impossible. She raised mostly all of her children in the projects, doing what she could to make ends meet. My mother made sure we all had a place to lay our heads. As an infant, my head in particular was in a dresser drawer, along with my two younger twin siblings, Sephora "Sophie" and Fifi. *We each had our own dresser drawer, of course.* It was the best my mother could do with what she had, which was only a two-bedroom apartment. The way my mother described it, she took the dresser drawers out of the dresser, laid a pillow in each drawer, and laid us on our backs so we didn't suffocate. Then she would put the makeshift bassinet next to her to watch us closely. My older siblings shared rooms and beds together while my mother slept in the living room with the twins and me. Through conversations with my mother, I learned that my mother had too many children to continue living in Raymond Rosen Projects, so we were forced to move, as the struggle continued to be real.

We moved (squatted) in another house on 30th & Clifford Street for about a year before my mother got caught. She was told the property was not a safe fit for our family. First, "the people" told her she had 30 days to find a place to live, or all of her children would be taken away from her and placed into foster care. Then, they had a change of heart, and told her that they would help her find housing. She had to take a seven-week course on how to paint, build small household things, and other important things a homeowner needed to know in order to maintain a house. My mother attended a class once a week for seven weeks, and was given my childhood home on 30th Street, between Lehigh and Huntingdon Streets. She was given the home for free for five years, not a dime (I wish I could live in a house free for five years). In those five years, she had to keep the house clean, up to date, and safe proof for all nine children plus the one who was in foster care and would eventually come to live with us in our home. It was a four-bedroom house that was three stories high with an unfinished basement. The basement was filled with dirt, like piles and piles of dirt, and it had a mildew smell. Two of the bedrooms were spacious, and two were small. There was a living room, a dining room, a kitchen, and a small but nice-sized backyard. When we first moved in, all nine of us were packed in our four-bedroom house comfortably.

My mother did everything she could and made it happen for her children. Three bedrooms had at least one set of bunk beds, where the top bunk was a twin, and the bottom bunk was a full-size bed, so that two or three people could sleep on the bottom bunk. I remember sleeping on the bottom bunk with the twins. It was kind of gross, considering we all wet the bed until we were like 13. We would all just be sleeping, tossing and turning in each other's piss, *ugh*, but we did what we had to do to survive. After the five years was up, my mother had to start paying a mortgage. She had to pay a monthly mortgage of $150 each month, using the government cash assistance she was receiving for each child. *My, how the cost of living was so low back in the day.* My mother was so driven to survive, keep and care for her children, that she doubled the monthly mortgage and paid it off completely by the time she was 45 years old. Although she was able to provide shelter for her children, my mother struggled to provide us with the appropriate emotional, mental, and physical support we needed. When things got hard for her as a single mother with 10 children, she began to use drugs and alcohol and abuse her children. Even in the state of what seemed like parental failure, my mother prayed to God for someone to take care of her children, because she wanted what's best for us.

North Filthadelphia

The streets of North Philadelphia took on the nickname of "North Filthadelphia," because the streets were always so dirty, and so were most of the people who resided in the area. I couldn't even walk down the streets without stepping over trash. I mean loads of trash like empty soda cans, plastic wrappings, drug casings, beer bottles, used condoms and so much more, all down the sidewalks and in the streets. People put their house trash out on the sidewalk days before the trash truck arrived, causing cats, squirrels, and other rodents to bite through the bag to eat, making a bigger mess of trash in the streets. The trash man only picked up the bags of trash, not the trash that is on the sidewalks and in the streets. There weren't any street sweeps in North Philly, so trash was just part of the neighborhood. Most blocks smelt horrible, like a dead rodent aroma that filled the air. Some blocks just smelt like trash, while other blocks smelt like poop. It was very seldom to walk on a block that just smelt like air. The sidewalks were unleveled and filled with cracks that could trip over. The streets were plagued with potholes that were so big, cars would have to drive on the sidewalk to get around them. Even the deep potholes were filled with trash. Children ran and played barefoot on the sidewalks and in the streets, making the bottom of their feet as black as tar. Many walked around with their hair all over the place and dirty clothes on their bodies.

Drug dealers were on every corner with their baggy jeans hanging past their butt cheeks, exposing their underwear to everyone, and they kept their hands in their underwear, *ewww*. They would smoke and drink, plucking their cigarette butts everywhere. Crackheads (males and females who were addicted to drugs) roamed up and down the streets. Most of them were very skinny, with bad skin and little to no clothes on their bodies. They stammered around asking people for money to buy "food" (drugs). There was a time when empty drug casings flooded the sidewalks of my neighborhood. The casings were small 1' or 2' clear cylinder like casings, with color tops. One day on my way to school, I stopped to pick one up and examine it, not knowing that it was a drug casing. Fifi slapped it out my hand saying, "Girl, that is a drug container. Don't touch that!" protecting me from my naivety. Thankfully there was nothing in the container because I may have tried it, and who knows what the rest of this story would be like, or if I would've even been around to tell my story. From that point on, I knew the streets were dangerous. There were gangs and shootings all over the neighborhood. This was not a good place to live, but I guess poor beggars can't be poor choosers.

This one hot summer day, the rest of my family and I were leaving the house to get into my mother's car when a blue car came dashing down our street. A group of cops swarmed our small block on 30th Street as they pursued the blue car in a high-speed chase. There were two people in the blue car, the driver and one passenger. As they flew down our block, the passenger threw a loaded rifle gun out of the window. I stood there astounded as I watched the gun slide under my neighbor's car. It was like I was watching an episode of "Cops," where the suspect was zooming down the street, except I wasn't watching TV, I was actually sitting right outside my house, watching the cops tailing on the blue car. My mother and everyone else who watched the incident unfold urged the rest of the neighborhood to go inside and lock their doors. I grabbed one of my sister's hands, and we ran in the house dropping to the floor just in case someone opened fire on the block. I was only nine years old, and I was so afraid. I understood enough about what was going on, and knew the routine to follow. Even the drug dealers on the corner dispersed. Those were just a few of the challenges I faced outside, but inside is where most of my challenges existed.

    My mother was a stickler for keeping a clean house. When I was a baby, my older sisters and brothers kept the house together. After they moved or ran away, my older siblings passed the baton to my younger sisters and me. I started cleaning the house as early as seven years old. By this time, it was four of us living with my mother, the last cycle of her children. The first thing I learned to do was clean my bed because I peed the bed for a long time. It was easy to clean because the plastic was still on the bed to prevent getting bed bugs, which we never got, surprisingly. When I would wet the bed, my mother would beat me and give me a bucket of water with White Cap Pine Oil. The Pine Oil masked the smell of a "pissy room" as my mother often yelled. Along with the bucket of water, she gave me an old cut up t-shirt to wipe the bed clean. My mother would wash my sheets by hand in the bathtub and hang them to dry on the clothes line in the backyard. By the time I was nine, I was cleaning the bathroom, vacuuming floors, and washing dishes. Cleaning the bathroom was the worst, *by the way, I love to clean now.* I had to scrub the woodwork (the base boards) with a toothbrush to make sure it was nice and clean. *Do you know how long it takes to clean woodwork with a toothbrush? Forever! No wonder it was Impossible to go outside and play because I was too busy playing young Cinderella (Did you see what I did there; Impossible & Cinderella, lol).* No matter how much I cleaned, it was never enough to keep bugs and rodents away.

I kept a clean house but those roaches and mice were everywhere. It seemed like the more I cleaned, the more the roaches and mice just kept multiplying. I guess because we lived in a row home, but it was annoying. My house was infested with roaches and mice!! There wasn't a safe space to go to doge a roach in the house. They were in my bed, on the walls, on the floor, in the refrigerator, *ugh I hate those things.* After cleaning the kitchen for the night and then turning on the kitchen light in the morning, there would be about twenty roaches on the countertops. As soon as I turned the lights on, the roaches would disperse and go into hiding in the cabinets and anywhere else they could go. Even when I was simply sitting down, I would feel roaches crawling down my arm, neck, or leg. Roaches are so disrespectful. They don't care where they go or who they land on. It got so bad I even knew when the roaches were about to have babies because they would have that little square brown thing hanging from the back of them, ready to deliver. *I can't believe I just wrote a whole paragraph about roaches. I am sorry to the readers who are roach sensitive, but next comes the mice.*

Truth be told, mice weren't a fear factor for me growing up. I actually didn't mind seeing them; I felt like they were my friends lol. *I sound like Michael Jackson, with his "pet mouse" Ben, (the mouse in his house).* In my house, there were mice everywhere. It didn't matter what time of day it was; they came out and made themselves like part of the family. They would just come out and run across my feet. If I was lying in the bed, one would run right across my head. I even had mice in the refrigerator. One day, I remember opening the refrigerator, only to find mice rummaging through the food. On another occasion, I remember opening the kitchen utensil drawer and finding 20 to 30 baby mice (pups). They were very tiny, pink, and translucent, and their eyes weren't quite developed yet. I showed my mother, and she pulled the whole drawer off the hinges and dumped it in a trash bag. (*Yes, the whole drawer!*) She then told me to walk it to the empty lot across the street. The lot was not a dumpster, but everyone on the block used it as a dumpster. I was so upset that my mother made me throw the pups in the trash. I started to cry as I was throwing out the bag. I already felt like I was leading the pups to their demise, just by telling my mother they existed. Disposing of them for my mother made me sad. Everyone in my house, except for me, was afraid of mice, which earned me the title "The Mice Buster." My mother was petrified of mice, dead or alive. If anyone saw a mouse, they would call me to come kill it, and if it was already dead, I would be called to dispose of the mouse. I can smell a dead mouse from anywhere; they have the worst smell when they are dead. Sometimes I would be in the house and my mother would ask what the foul smell was, and I would answer, "It's a dead mouse." Then I would go on a hunt to find the dead rodent. When I found it, I would get a piece of toilet paper and pick up the mouse by its tail, take it to the bathroom, and flush it down the toilet. No matter how much I cleaned, I had roaches and mice. Although I tried to keep a clean house, I was still a product of "North Filthadelphia," and my life reflected as such.

A Product of my Environment

On average, I thought I was a good child, but I was definitely a product of my environment. I learned how to steal from my sister Lyfe, and my mother and a few of my older sisters smoked cigarettes and drank alcohol. My mother never really hid her smoking and drinking habits. There were clear glass ashtrays filled with old cigarette butts and ashes in the living room and in my mother's room. She smoked in front of me every day and would tell me to empty the ashtrays at times. It was inevitable for me to become a thieving smoker and a drinker because that was all the norm.

I was about nine when I first learned how to steal. Lyfe was a pro at it, so she taught me everything she knew about stealing. It all started when we were sneaking out after my mother left the house. We snuck and went to the pool to swim. There was a pool in Mander Playground that we would sneak off to often. The pool didn't have any clothing rules, like you literally could swim in a shirt and shorts; which was good for my sisters and I because we didn't have swim clothes; but most people had swim suits. Those people would take off their street clothes and lay them on the ground or on the benches if there were any. While they were in the pool having a good time, my sister Lyfe, Fifi and I would go around checking pockets for money. Lyfe taught me to get in the pool for a little bit, come out and check pockets, give her the money and then get back in the pool. It worked all the time, I never got caught stealing at the pool. I then graduated from stealing from people at the pool to stealing from stores. Lyfe taught me how to go into stores with just enough money to buy one small thing and steal other things at the same time. It made me look less suspicious when I bought something. It worked most of the times, I would steal chips, cakes, drinks and candy. I got caught a few times, got chased out of a few stores by security and owners of the Poppy stores, but never booked for stealing. I didn't have a conscious about stealing then, I never really felt convicted for stealing. My only conscious was not to get caught by my mother, because that would be perilous times. I mostly continued to steal when I was hungry and my mother wasn't going to be home to cook.

My oldest sister Trina introduced me to my first drink and cigarette. When I was eight years old, my sisters and I visited Trina at the projects she lived in, in South Philly. We didn't visit Trina much, but whenever we did, there were no rules and no bedtimes. One night Trina, Lyfe, Fifi and I were sitting outside, along with a few of Trina's friends. They were smoking and drinking, and Trina was letting Lyfe and Fifi do the same.

She nudged me and said, "Here little sis, take a swig." It was a cold can of Olde English 800.

I took a swig and spit it out immediately saying, "Ugh, this is disgusting," as I wiped my hand across my mouth to clean off the remnant of beer left on my mouth and chin.

Trina smacked me upside my head, saying, "Girl, don't waste my shit, take another swig!"

I took another swig as I was told and did not waste one bit. Before I swallowed, I held the bitter libation in my mouth for a minute, to prepare myself for the nastiness going down my throat. After I swallowed the beer, Trina passed me the cigarette she was smoking. "Take a puff," she said. I took the cigarette from Trina, grabbed it and placed it between my thumb and index finger, put the brown part in my mouth, and inhaled deeply. I coughed so much that I thought my lungs were going to come out. It felt like I was choking on air, my eyes were watering and everything. *I still remember the pain I felt when I inhaled that cigarette. Cigarettes hurt to inhale for some reason.* "Damn, little sis, easy," Trina laughed, while patting my back and swatting the smoke away from my face. "Don't tell Mommy I let y'all smoke and drink with me, or she gonna kick all our asses," Trina said jokingly but seriously. "Oh, I won't!" I replied with the quickness, talking through my coughs.

    Smoking and drinking became part of the norm for me since its introduction by Trina. My mother always had beer in the fridge, which was mainly Colt 45. Although I didn't like the taste of beer, I still drank it occasionally when my mother left unfinished beer in the fridge. There were packs of Newport Short cigarettes in the living room where my mother sat most of the time. When she wasn't looking, Lyfe would bribe me to take a cigarette and stash it away until my mother left the house.

"Go get a cigarette from the living room while Mommy is in the kitchen," Lyfe said to me one day.

"I don't want to, you do it, Lyfe," I responded.

"If you don't get that cigarette, I am going to tell Mommy about that boy you kissed on the playground," Lyfe said black mailing me.

Although I was too afraid to get caught stealing, I was more afraid of getting in trouble for kissing a boy, so I did as I was told. Fifi was the lookout most of the time so I wouldn't get caught. Luckily, I never got caught stealing my mother's cigarettes, but I did get caught smoking her cigarettes.

Lyfe, Fifi, and I usually climbed out of my bedroom window to smoke cigarettes on the roof. It was our way of not getting the smell of smoke in the house while my mother wasn't home. One day, Lyfe, Fifi and I decided to just open the window and smoke cigarettes from inside the house, but blow the smoke outside the window. We weren't smart enough to know that any breeze from the outside could blow the smoke back into the house. I heard my mother's car come down the street. I ran into my mother's front bedroom to see if it was her car, and it was. I ran back to my room in a panic, my heart beating 1,000 beats per minute.

"Quick, Mommy is here, close the window," I whispered loudly. I started to swat the air trying to clear up the smoke. "Go wash your hands and put toothpaste in your mouth," Lyfe whispered to Fifi and me.

I quickly ran into the bathroom, put toothpaste on my finger and rubbed my finger across my teeth back and forth, adding water and squishing it around my mouth, gargling, doing whatever I could to get the smell of smoke out of my mouth. I thought the plan was genius, until it wasn't genius.

My mother walked into the house and yelled up the steps, "What is that smell?" It was like she had a super smelling sense or something. *I guess she would because she smoked enough cigarettes to recognize the smell a mile away.* Not understanding that I was being used as bait, Fifi convinced me to go downstairs and answer my mother so everyone didn't get in trouble.

I ran down the stairs and said, "Ma'am?"

"You didn't hear me, what is that smell? It smells like cigarette smoke."

My mother quickly smacked my chest while she grabbed the front of my shirt, balled up in her fist, and sniffed it. *Shit, I didn't think about changing my shirt,* I thought.

"You smoking in my house," my mother yelled with her face touching my face.

"No ma'am," I lied.

"So, now you are just gonna lie in my face too, hunh?" she said, pushing me away.

I fell to the floor crying. Meanwhile, Lyfe and Fifi never came downstairs to see what was going on until my mother called for them.

She yelled up the stairs "Lyfe, Pheonix, get down here now!"

"Ma'am", both Lfye and Fifi answered as they made their way down the stairs.

"So yall in here smoking in my house!"

"No Ma'am, not me" Lyfe lied, as if she had absolutely nothing to do with us smoking.

My mother grabbed Fifi, tossing over to where I was and walked away to get a belt. She whipped Fifi and I for smoking in her house, letting Lyfe off the hook, as usual. Even though I got caught smoking, it didn't stop me from smoking, it just stopped me from getting caught. I was officially a product of my environment.

The Block

30th Street was in the middle of the hood, but it was a great little community of its own. The children on the block got along with one another, as did the adults, and everyone protected each other. The block was family.

There were so many children who lived on the block, from infants to adult children, still living in their parents' home, but we all got along well for the most part. Whenever I walked home from school or to the corner store, the kids on the block would say hi and ask if I could come out to play. *Kids can be persistent because they knew darn well, I couldn't come out to play.* I would say, "I can't. I have to do something" or sometimes tell the flat-out truth: "My mom won't let me come out today. I'm on punishment." Sometimes I would ask one of my friends to ask my mom if we could come out, thinking she would say yes to my friends and say no to me, but it almost never worked. When I was able to go outside or when I snuck outside, I had a good time with my friends on the block. We'd jump rope, play ball, and race up and down the block, from one pole to the next. It was fun playing with the kids on my block until I had to fight a few of them one day.

I had this one friend who lived at the top of the block, across the street from me who liked me. His name was Julio, and he was 11 years old. At the time, Julio was 500 pounds, and he had special needs. The kids on the block did tease him a little, but I was his only real friend. His mother, Ms. Sheila, asked me if I could help Julio walk, so he could lose weight. Julio hated walking, but he liked me so much that I was able to talk him into walking. Ms. Sheila asked my mother if I could walk with Julio up and down the block a few times every day, and my mother obliged. *This was one way I was able to go outside and get fresh air for a little bit after school each day, so I capitalized on it.* I did like helping Julio in the process.

Julio got so attached to me that he started calling me his girlfriend. As we walked down the street, he yelled to people, "This is my girlfriend!" He had a very loud voice and was very talkative. The kids on the block sang "Julio and Meena, sitting in the tree, K-I-S-S-I-N-G!" I was so embarrassed, but I knew he had special needs, so I just played along with it to avoid hurting his feelings. Julio was a great kid, and otherwise fun to be around. We played board games on his step before our walks. He was part of the block, so I looked out for Julio. Julio died two years later from obesity. He was 700 pounds when he died at the age of 13.

One hot summer day while my mother wasn't home, my sisters and I snuck outside. Fifi, Sophie, and I sat on the porch. We weren't even leaving the porch because we didn't want to get caught if my mother drove down the block. It was easier to stay on the porch with the door wide open, just in case we had to hurry and run in the house when we heard my mother's car. This one particular day, a few of the boys on the block—Slim, Rob and Meek, *("The Squad" is what they called themselves, so original, right?)* who were all around Lyfe's age, about 14-16. Meek was 14, and he was the thickest out of the three; he wasn't fat, but he wasn't skinny, either. He was light skinned with nice teeth and a nice smile. Slim was the oldest; he was 16 and the tallest and the darkest of the three. He was really annoying to be around; all he did was talk about how he got money and girls. Rob was 14 as well, and he was the quiet boy; he wasn't too short, but he wasn't tall, and he was a brown skin color. They were playing on the porch with my sisters and me. We were all running back and forth on the small porch. The boys started jumping over the railing of my porch and running up the stairs. They were doing too much. Sophie was sitting on the top steps watching us play until Meek jumped over Sophie's head. Sophie sat with her back facing the front door as she looked toward the sidewalk. When Meek jumped over Sophie's head, he kicked her in the back of the head by accident. *Even though he shouldn't have jumped over her head in the first place.* Sophie went tumbling down the six stairs onto the sidewalk.

"Oh shit!" Meek said after he realized he knocked Sophie down the stairs.

"Oh my God, why would you jump over her head like that?" I shouted at Meek.

"It was an accident! I thought I could make it!" Meek shouted back.

"You about to be in an accident in a minute!" Fifi shouted.

Meanwhile, Sophie was on the ground crying. "Pick her up!" Fifi shouted to Meek. Sophie was very heavy to carry; since she couldn't walk, it was like carrying dead weight. Meek, Slim, and Rob picked Sophie up together. Meek grabbed her from behind under her arms, Slim grabbed her legs, and Rob directed them into the house.

The boys carried Sophie into the house and sat her down in her wheelchair. Sophie's lip was busted and knuckles were all scratched up.

"Oh, my God, look at her lip. We gonna get our asses beat for this!" Fifi yelled.

Meek answered, "Look, I'm gonna go get her a popsicle that she can keep on it to help the swelling go down." I could tell Meek was afraid because his voice was a little shaky. He ran to the corner store and got Sophie the long, thick 50 cent blue popsicle. When he came back, he gave the popsicle to Sophie and quickly ran back outside without saying sorry. Fifi yelled, "So, you not gonna apologize to my sister?"

"Yo, I just bought her a popsicle, of course I'm sorry," Meek said, running down the steps. Without a word spoken, Fifi and

I followed Meek down the stairs and started beating on him. I was on the right side of Meek while Fifi was on the left, and we were going blow for blow. "Apologize to my sister," Fifi yelled over and over, blow after blow. He fell to the ground, so we started kicking him. Afterward, I pulled him up against a car, and Fifi and I started giving him body shots. The boys didn't even try to help Meek. I don't think they ever saw us fight before. I grabbed Meek by his shirt and pulled him up the stairs and back into the house so he could apologize to Sophie, and he did so in pain and with sincerity. After that, we were friends again, and the block continued to look out for each other.

A few weeks later, my sister Isabella got into a fight with a girl from her school. Isabella wasn't a fighter, but she wasn't no punk either. My sisters and I were in the house when this girl Manita knocked on the door for Isabella. My mother wasn't home at the time.

My sister Lyfe answered the door, "Who is it?"

"Open the door and you will see!" Manita responded with an attitude.

Lyfe opened the door, and Manita started yelling, "Where your sister at? Bring her ass out here!"

There were three girls with Manita at the bottom of the steps. The teenagers on our block were alerted by the noise, and they all came running to our house. The girls on the block rushed through Manita and her crew as if to say, "Is there a problem?" Manita started talking all this trash about how she wanted to fight Isabella. That's when "The Block" stepped in, the girls on the block made it so Manita's posse would stay out the fight so that Isabella and Manita could have a fair fight.

Isablella went inside the house to put some Vaseline on her face, *because she was light skinned and that's what light skinned people did when they didn't want to get their face messed up.* She came back outside, and the girls on the block had Manita waiting in the street, while they were standing in front of Manita's friends making sure they didn't jump in the fight. Isabella came down the stairs, walked into the street and took the first punch. I was scared because Isabella was the nicest sister I had; I didn't know if she could fight or not. She took the first punch, Manita hit back, and they were going back and forth for a little while. Isabella was winning the fight, *I tell you, we were some fighting girls.* The girls on the block broke up the fight, pushing them and calling them names, and the three girls scurried away. The block was always looking out for us.

The adults on the block were very friendly, neighborly, and watchful over all the children. In the mornings when I left for school, some neighbors who were out would say, "Be good at school." My neighbor, Ms. Marie, who was a few houses down from mine, frequently asked my mother for sugar, milk, or salt if she needed it, and if my mother had it, she would give it to Ms. Marie. I don't remember my mother ever asking my neighbors for anything, but she was always willing to give. On nice days, the adults would be sitting outside on their porches, talking to each other or gossiping about people or people's kids. My mother didn't really engage in many conversations with a lot of the neighbors, but she did have one neighbor she talked to almost every day, Ms. Neetchi. My mother and Ms. Neetchi often hung out together all night.

My mother let me help this older woman who lived directly across the street from me. The lady was Ms. Jane who lived alone. Ms. Jane was in her 60's at the time. She was very thin with a hunched back. Sometimes I would see her walking from the store with a lot of bags in her hands. Whenever I saw her carrying bags, I would run over to her and help her. She gave me dollars for helping. One day, Ms. Jane walked over to my house and asked my mother if I could walk her to the store so I could help her carry her groceries. My mother allowed me, *which was another breath of fresh air for me.* I would walk Ms. Jane to the store about twice a week, and she would give me a few dollars. I never told my mother about the money because I didn't want her to take it or tell me to give it back, and I never got caught.

I loved going shopping with Ms. Jane until a few months later when she fell. This one time I walked her to Save a Lot on 29th and Huntingdon Street. We made it in the store, grabbed what she needed, and placed it in the shopping cart. Ms. Jane paid for her food at the register, and we walked out of the store to head home. Ms. Jane and I were walking down the street about a block away from Save a Lot, and two blocks away from the house, Ms. Jane trips. I was walking ahead of Ms. Jane on the left side of her when I saw a part of the concrete that wasn't leveled. I didn't think I needed to tell Ms. Jane to watch her step because I thought she saw it. I thought, *if I saw it then, she must have seen it,* but I was wrong, obviously. Ms. Jane didn't see that the sidewalk was uneven and didn't step high enough over the level of the concrete and fell to the ground.

Ms. Jane fell straight on her knees and then on her face, busting her lip and banging up her knees. Her bags fell on the sides of her. I felt so bad and afraid at the same time. I was only 11 and wasn't strong enough to help get her up off the ground with her bags. Thankfully, a guy who walked past us was able to help, *something I didn't see much in North Philly, a gentleman.* He grabbed Ms. Jane by her right arm, and I grabbed her left as she struggled to get back on her feet. Ms. Jane was whining a little bit, but not fully crying. "Oooooooh, oooooooh," she said as she kept touching her lip. "I'm so sorry, Ms. Jane!" I explained.

"Oh baby, no worries, you didn't see that crack in the ground," she said, still holding on to her lips.

I know I saw it, but I never said a word about seeing it because I didn't want to get in trouble. I helped dust Ms. Jane off, helped her pick up her bags, and held her hand the rest of the way home.

The Mystery House

The house to the right of me was abandoned for as long as I can remember. It was the only house on my side of the block without a porch. It was a mysterious house that had three stories like mine, but painted all white with yellow awnings over the front bedroom. For some reason FiFi and I were so obsessed with this house. We wondered, *why is the house empty? Is it clean, or dirty? Why is it the only house on the block without a porch? How can we get in there to find out?* Even though we knew it wasn't right to break into an abandoned house, we still had to find out its mystery. *Maybe this is why Fifi and I always got in trouble together, because we did some dumb stuff.* We even thought about the consequences if our mother found out.

"She's just gonna beat the shit out of us," FiFi said.

I chimed in, "She gonna do that anyway, so we may as well make it good!"

One day we decided to become detectives and solve the mystery of the abandoned house.

One early summer afternoon, my mother wasn't home, as usual. Lyfe was in charge, but she left Fifi, Sophie , and me home, while she went to do whatever she wanted. Fifi and I had time to think of a plan on how we would get in the house next door.

"I don't even think the door is going to be open. That would be stupid," I said to Fifi.

She responded, "Well, maybe a window is open or something. We should still try."

"What about Sophie?" I asked Fifi.

"We can't bring her; we would have to carry her and we would definitely get caught," Fifi answered.

Sophie chimed in, "I can be the lookout, just in case Mommy comes back home. I will knock on the wall so y'all know to come back over."

Sophie was good at finding quick solutions to Fifi's and my shenanigans. The decision was final; we left Sophie in the house alone as the lookout. Sophie was our lookout many times before, for our different escapades.

We knew we couldn't go through the front of the house because then the kids on the block who played outside would be able to see us. Once they saw us they would tell their parents, and their parents would tell our mother, and our mother would beat the crap out of us when she got home, and that would not be good. So, we decided to go to the backyard to see if there was a way in. We lived in a row house, so the abandoned house was connected to ours; there was no space between the two houses. There was a fence that separated our backyards from each other. There were two ways we could get into the house — the first being from the roof, as I could easily climb out of my bedroom window onto the roof and walk to the bedroom of the abandoned house. The second option would be to climb the fence in the backyard and try the back door to get in the house. We tried the latter because it was more fun and mysterious to perform. We weren't able to get out much unless we were sneaking out, so this was perfect. We could sneak out and still be super close to the house. Fifi climbed the fence first, and I followed. We didn't think about who would try the door first, so we played rock-paper-scissors to see who would be the lucky winner. "Rock, paper, scissors shoot!" we both chanted, pounding one balled up fist onto the other flat open hand. At first, I beat Fifi with a rock because she had chosen scissors, then she said, "Best two out of three," with some madness in her voice. We played again, and Fifi won with scissors because I had paper, and then Fifi won the last round with paper because I chose the rock. Fifi balled my rock up so fast with her paper hand and squeezed, "Un Ha, I beat ya, follow me sucka." Not wasting any time, Fifi grabbed the door knob and turned it to the right and pushed, but just before she could open the door, I had to say, "Just to let you know, I actually won rock-paper-scissors first." Fifi answered, "It doesn't matter how you started, I finished it with the win, now come on!" Fifi continued to push the door, and the door opened. "It's unlocked!" we both whispered to each other. Excited and skittish, we both took in a big gasp of air . We didn't know what was going to be on the other side of the door, so we tiptoed in quietly, closing the door gently behind us.

The house was definitely vacant. Fifi and I walked through the kitchen, and there was nothing; neither a stove nor a refrigerator, no cabinets no nothing, just gray drywall with white spots of paint. As we walked through the downstairs and then the upstairs, the only thing that was in the house was wooden planks of different sizes, dirt, and spider webs with spiders in the corners. I noticed the spiders because I am petrified of spiders; I have a Spidey sense when it comes to spiders. My senses tingle when they are around, and it makes me go on a spider search. I needed to know that they are around and decide whether I could continue with our shenanigans. The spiders were just in the corners so I could deal with them, as long as one did not move. Normally, once I see a spider start to move around, I am aborting the plan in a flash. This house was too mysterious, so I had to stick to the plan. As soon as I saw a spider, I made a plan of how I was going to kill it if one decided to crawl out of their corner. I was going to take off both shoes and clap it really hard between the shoes. If the spider fell, I was going to stomp it until it disappeared, but none of them moved, so I was good.

We did not go in the basement because the basement in our own house was nothing but dirt, junk, lots of spiders and spider webs. We imagined the same for the abandoned basement. The house was just big enough for the two of us to run around and do whatever we wanted to do in an empty house. After touring the downstairs, we tiptoed upstairs as each wooden step creaked. The house had the same layout as my house; even the creaking steps, so it felt like home. Fifi and I walked through all four rooms upstairs, and saw nothing but a little dust. The house was officially empty and available for use by the two of us, as we started a game of tag. After we played a few rounds, we pretended to watch TV in one of the rooms that was in the same place as our bedroom in our house. My mother had a TV in her room that we used to sneak and watch when she wasn't home before she put a lock on her door and locked it every time she left the house. So, we pretended to be in our own room watching TV.

"What should we watch?" I asked in a calm, leisurely voice.

"Let's watch Barney!" Fifi said excitedly.

We watched Barney on our imaginary TV, as we sang Barney songs and danced around the room having a good time.

"This is like our own tree house, except it's not in a tree. It's our playhouse," I said to Fifi.

"Just keep this between me, you and Sophie. If Lyfe finds out about this, she is going to steal our playhouse and then tell Mommy," Fifi responded.

Fifi and I shook on it. That was the first time we had anything to ourselves without Lyfe having a hand in it and holding it over our heads as blackmail.

Our daily trips to our playhouse continued for weeks before we got caught by my mother one day. Fifi and I played different games, and our imagination grew stronger as we imagined we were different people in different places. Sometimes we took some things from our house like sheets and blankets and used them for games and pretend play. One day Sophie knocked on the wall, but neither Fifi nor I heard the knock right away. By the time we first heard the knock, we were upstairs in the playhouse, and it was too late. My mother was already downstairs calling to us from our real house. Fifi and I climbed out of the room window of the play house that was next to our bedroom window onto the roof, opened our window and climbed through. I went through the window first, then Fifi, and as soon as Fifi got her last foot through the window my mother was entering our room, and it went down.

"Why are you coming through the window, Fifi?" my mother yelled.

"No ma'am, I didn't come through the window," Fifi answered with a straight but not so straight face, hoping my mother didn't see much.

"So, you telling me you didn't just climb through that window? I just watched you do it! So now I am a blind liar!" my mother started to yell.

It was very hard to tell how much my mother saw because when I came through the window, I didn't see her; I had my back turned trying to help Fifi through the window. I stood there quietly, hoping she would not ask me any questions.

"Tameena, did you see Fifi just climb through that window?" my mother asked with her hands on her hip and a tight lip.

"No ma'am, Fifi did not climb through the window." I lied regretfully.

My mother grabbed Fifi and me, and she started whooping our behinds. She gave us a speech while she beat us. With each strike she said one word like "You (strike)-gone (strike) -sit (strike)-in (strike) -my (strike) -face (strike)-and (strike) -lie (strike)!" she screamed out of breath. My mother must have said a whole paragraph before she finished beating us; it was one of our longest beatings. We started out by the window and winded up cornered in the tiny closet in our room, getting punched all over our bodies. The closet had to be about six feet long. Fifi and I were just all on top of each other trying to share the licks.

The Good Times

The good times are what always kept me close to her, even when they were outweighed by the bad times. I loved my mother, and I still love my mother. It did not matter what my mother did to me, how much she beat me, how afraid of her I became, I still loved and needed her, as all children need their parents. To the reader, if you are like me in any way reading this book, try to remember the good times you had with your loved ones who have done you wrong. I'm not saying it's okay for what they have done to you, but I am saying it's okay to remember the good. I take solace in remembering the good times and I encourage you to do the same. It helps with the forgiving process. Yeah, I know you may be thinking of all the horrible things your loved ones have done to you, and how messed up you may be now because of it, but remember the good times you had together, as this may help you in your healing process; I know it's helping me.

When my mother was sober, she was a "good parent," whatever that is defined as, considering there is no written rule book on what to do and what not to do as a parent. She took my siblings and me to the playground, gave us money, and even was a little silly at times. There was a playground behind the school I attended, Rhodes Middle School, a block away from our house that we couldn't go to because there was always something bad happening. Despite the violence and chaos that took place in our house, my mother wanted to shield us from the violence and chaos of the community outside our house. Instead, she took us to Mander Playground, which was around the corner from us on 33rd street. We would get up early and get dressed for the day ahead. Most of the time my mother would dress Fifi, Sophie, and me as triplets because we were less than a year apart. Fifi and Sophie were fraternal twins, so they didn't look totally alike. They were born a month before my first birthday. I still *wonder about that sometimes, like really Mom, did I even get to have a 1st birthday party?* Even though Sophie and Fifi are twins, Sophie and I look identical to each other, so much that many people thought we were twins or that the three of us were triplets. I guess that's why my mother dressed us as triplets. In fact, Sophie and I looked so much alike, the only difference between us is that she is in a wheelchair, and I can walk. Even with that big distinction, when people would see me separated from my sister, some would ask, "Wait, weren't you in a wheelchair?" or "You can walk now?" as if some miracle had been performed. Anyway, my mother was so talented she would sew some of our clothes. She would buy fabric and sew them into matching outfits. One time, the three of us went to the playground dressed in Dick Tracy comic fabric. That was my favorite outfit to wear. It was a short set, which included a white shirt with a picture of Dick Tracy on the front, and blue shorts with different comic speech bubbles. These outfits my mother made were the closest to new we ever got. I believe the reason why they were my favorite was because I was the first owner of those outfits. After getting dressed, we went off to the playground. The playground was really big; it had a pool, a few swing sets, monkey bars, and other things to play in, and a lot of grassy space to run around and have fun. Sometimes when my mother received her food stamps, she would buy so much food and bring it to the park so we could have a cookout. She would buy different meats like hot dogs, hamburgers, chicken and spare ribs, *even though I don't eat much of that stuff now, my mouth waters remembering the taste of a good ole BBQ.* While my mom cooked on the grill, we would be running around having fun. Although we could have played with other children at the playground, there were seven to ten of us, so we didn't need any friends. We could just play amongst ourselves and have fun. Ah, those were the good ole days, days that seemed carefree for children.

    I remember the times when my mother got her food stamps, she would give me two dollars to get junk food and candy from the corner store. At this time, there were a lot of us: my three sisters, my two nieces, my nephew, and me. She gave the money to me although my older sister Lyfe walked us to the store. My older sister was still learning how to count because of her intellectual disability, and she stole, so I had to be the responsible one and report back to my mother. At the store we would all pick out things that everyone liked so that we could share. Back then two dollars could get you a lot of snacks; we got chips, cakes and candy for just two dollars. See, a bag of chips was 25 cents, cakes were 25 cents, and you could buy candy for a penny. Whenever we bought cakes, I always made sure to get the kind that had two in a pack, such as Donut Sticks, Twinkies, or my personal favorite, Jelly Rolls, because those could be split between us. We never bought anything to drink because we were okay with drinking sugar water in the house. *Ugh, I can't believe we actually drank that*, but we were so happy. Once we got back home, we would empty all of the bags onto the floor and marvel at all of our junk, and then dig in to eat. My mother would join in sometimes and eat with us, but most of the time she let us indulge in our junk desires. We were a happy family once upon a time, from what my little mind thought was happiness at that time. Sometimes we would sit and eat dinner at the table together as a family. At the table my mom would tell us to eat our "dookie balls" (Brussels sprouts) that no one liked, which I guess was her way of getting us to eat? Although it made me not want to eat it more, the table was filled with so much laughter because of the word "dookie." None of us liked them but for some reason, it made it easier for us to eat when they were dookie balls.

There were times when we watched movies in my mother's room. We all piled up in my mother's queen-sized bed, snuggled under the covers watching scary movies together until we fell asleep. We all loved scary movies back then, but now for some reason as an adult, I can't watch scary movies. My mother's favorite scary show was *Tales from the Crypt*. It was a spooky show with some type of old, decomposing human looking character named The Crypt Keeper. The Crypt Keeper was ugly and wrinkly with long, thin gray hair, so thin you could see his scalp. It had big beady blue eyes, a missing nose, and rotten teeth, *at least the teeth he had left*. When it laughed, it made spooky witch sounding noises! My mother would be silly and say, "Ooh, he is so cute, I want to marry him." We would all laugh and make jokes about how cute the ugly Crypt Keeper looked, and she did the same with Freddy Krueger, The Boogie Man, Michael Myers and other scary ugly characters, but the Crypt Keeper was her favorite. This one time we watched the movie *It*, the one that came out in 1990, not the remake. *The older one is scarier in my opinion.* This movie scared all of us so much, but it scared Sophie more.

We were in my mother's room watching it when Sophie covered her ears and said, "I don't want to see it!"

"Well cover your eyes because you can still see it if you're holding your ears," I replied laughing.

Sophie covered her eyes and said, "I don't want to hear it either!"

"Well cover your ears, Sophie!" I said laughing hysterically.

Everyone burst into laughter, and it's still as funny now as it was then. We loved to watch movies as a family.

    I remember being able to play outside on the block. Even though we weren't able to do it as often as the other kids, I still remember. As long as we stayed in front of the house and on the sidewalk, we were good. The street was always forbidden and we didn't dare try it because we all knew what would follow. The only time we were able to play in the street was when we had a block party. Our block parties were so much fun. Every year on the 4th of July, which also happens to be my mother's birthday, we had a block party. It was something I looked forward to every year. Someone on the block always bought a birthday cake for my mom. After everyone on the block put their tents up, fired up the grills, and before extended family members showed up and the music started, the whole block would sing happy birthday to my mom. Everyone on the block would get a slice of cake and enjoy the block party. Mr. Point, who lived across the street diagonally, was the DJ. He had a great big black rectangular speaker that he put in the middle of the street. His music was bumping, and we danced and sang along to songs he played. Oh, and I was a great dancer; I'd like to think I still am minus the bad knees, but I always won the dancing contests at the block parties. Mr. Point would start the music, and I would get to dancing. Mr. Point was just that — he was on point. He was the best DJ ever, who happened to be the only one I knew at the time, anyway. We would jump rope, play king ball, ride bikes, (Well, the other kids rode their bikes; we didn't have bikes.) race, and have a great time, all in the middle of the street. During these block parties, all of my neighbors cooked on their grills while others ate from anywhere on the block. There was so much food, snacks, alcoholic beverages, and lots of candy for children. It was like one big, happy block family. When it got dark, someone would bring out the glow sticks that every child wore around their necks, wrists, and/or ankles. I had so much fun. It was the only time we were able to stay out all day and night, even if we were always the first family to go in the house for the night.

There were some good times in the house; even when my mother was drunk, she would blast oldies in the house. My mother had a wooden record player and stand with built-in speakers she kept in the living room that she would play every once in a while. She had to have over 50 vinyl record discs of different artists. Some of the discs were different sizes —7,10, and 12 inch discs that my mother organized by size. The size of the disc determined how much music you were able to play on each side of the record, the lowest inch being the least amount of music to the highest inch being the most amount of music that played. Each side could play three to five songs on either side of the record. The discs were round and black with the center a different color based on the artist's title and style. She would take the disc out of the rectangular cardstock cover and handle the record very carefully to avoid getting it dirty with fingerprints. She carried it by each end of the record pressed against the palm of her hands that were straight out, with her thumbs pointing up, not letting her fingers touch the record at all. Ever so gently, my mother placed the vinyl record on the record player to prepare it for making music. Then, she took the long silver line thingy carefully, and carefully placed it on top of the disc, so the disc could stay on track and not get scratched. If the disc got scratched, the music would skip and the whole record would be destroyed. I always wondered why she would say, "Don't touch my records or I will break your fingers!" It was a lot of work that went into the process of playing music. Let's face it, whether I understood the reason or not, I believed she meant every word she said, and I never tried it, that's for sure. No one in the house was allowed to touch any part of that record player except my mother; or else, the good times would be over in a flash. Finally, the moment I always looked forward to: The record started to spin, and the music started to play.

My mom would lip sync, and sometimes sing aloud, grabbing my sisters and me to sing along. We would dance and sing in circles with our balled-up fists as microphones and have a great time. I loved to sing; I still do, and I was good at it. My favorite song to sing was "I Wish It Would Rain" by The Temptations. Although the song is about a girl who left a man, and the sadness it brought him made him want to cry, it was how I felt about my family. He couldn't cry because he was a man, and men didn't cry. He wished that it would rain so he could hide his tears in the rain. My favorite part was "My eyes search the skies desperately for rain, Cause raindrops will hide my teardrops, and no one will ever know that I'm crying, crying, crying when I go outside…I wish it would rain, oooh, ooooh." Looking back on the lyrics, it's so profound; it expressed how I felt then, and sometimes how I feel now. Still to this day I like to cry in the shower because in the shower I don't have to give an explanation of my feelings to anyone.

Music was and is my life line. I'm so glad my mother introduced me to music; those were the good times.

We also went to camp. The social services agency that was working with my family paid for us to go to camp. Only Fifi, Sophie, and I went to camp. Lyfe couldn't go because she had sickle cell, and my mother did not want her to have a crisis moment away at camp. Camp was so much fun; it was a time that we could get away from the craziness for one whole week during the summer. Sometimes we went two or three times during the summer. It was an overnight Christian camp called "Camp Indian Run." We learned about the Bible and God. We sang worship songs around the fire while roasting marshmallows. Actually, camp is where I accepted The Lord Jesus Christ in my life for the first time (I got saved). I remember that day like it was yesterday. I was in Chapel and we were singing "Take My Hand, Precious Lord," and the lyrics made me so emotional that tears started to flow from my eyes. *I was crying in front of people y'all*. A camp counselor came to me and asked me if I wanted to give my life to the Lord. I think she assumed the reason for my tears was because I wanted to know the Lord better, but my tears were because I didn't want to go home to be a punching bag. There was no way I would be able to tell her my story of what was going on at home. I let her assume, and after a back-and-forth conversation about what it meant, I said yes with tears flowing from my eyes. Just like that I was saved (born again), and I believe that God has been watching over me ever since. *I seem to have gotten a little off topic there; where was I? Oh yeah,* we would go swimming every day and play different types of sports and games at camp. My favorite part of camp was when we had swimming games at night. It would be dark, and the counselors would turn the pool lights on and have all the campers stand around the perimeter of the pool, with their backs facing the water. The counselors would throw small water containers filled with different amounts of money in the pool. When they blew their whistle, we had to turn around, jump in the pool and find as many containers as we could. The best part is we actually got to keep the money and use it at camp for whatever we had enough to buy. Considering my mother sent us to camp with no money, I made it my business to find as many containers as I could to get some money for my sisters and myself. Sometimes I found a total of five to 10 dollars, and if my sisters found any money, we would split it between us all. The other campers were nice, and the best thing of all, Fifi and I never got in trouble. I still can't believe we made it a whole week without fighting with anyone. It was like the camp counselors kept us so busy learning about Jesus and having fun, that we didn't have time to act out or start trouble with anyone. Another thing I loved most about going to camp, was that the camp was wheelchair accessible for Sophie, so she got to have fun like Fifi and me. Sophie even got the chance to get in the pool at camp. She was the first one to get in and collect two containers. Oftentimes when we did things, Sophie felt left out because it may not have been wheelchair accessible, but camp was awesome, even for Sophie. It was the best week of our lives each summer we went.

    I can't forget the times when Fifi, Sophie and I went "ice skating" in the bathtub. My mother didn't know about this because we always did it when she wasn't home, but it was so much fun. So, what happened was, I would run water, wetting the whole tub. Next, Fifi would get a bar of soap, lather it up and coat the entire tub. After we made the tub nice and soapy, we would get undressed, wet ourselves with water, and then lather ourselves with the bar of soap. *Just typing this brings laughter to my soul.* Then all three of us would get our soapy selves in the tub and just roll, slide, and skate around the tub. At first, we all skated around the tub together at the same time, slipping and falling all over each other, but then realized we could take turns so that we each could get the best out of the activity, and to make sure we didn't hurt Sophie. I don't know what made us think of this, but we made fun out of what we had in our means. Inspiration of this activity may have come to pass, because the three of us used to take baths together, *why would three people share a bath? Three dirty people.* Thinking back on this, it was very disgusting; three dirty little nine and 10-year old girls taking a bath together, in a 6-foot long, 3-foot wide bathtub, sitting in murky water, *ewww.* We would have to sit in the tub criss-cross applesauce, splashing each other with water until it was time to wash our bodies. Yeah, it was nasty, but it was so much fun to have a bond with my sisters in that way. I'm so glad I can remember the good times.

Daddy Issues

From what I was told when I became an adult, my father was around in the early years of my life. So early, I can't remember much about him. My mother showed me pictures of my daddy holding me when I was first born. According to the pictures, I learned that my daddy was tall and skinny like me. He had a caramel brown skinned complexion with reddish brown hair. I saw different pictures of him holding me until I was three years old. Each picture I saw were happy family pictures. There were pictures of birthday cakes and Christmas trees with presents under them (very few presents, but at least I saw them in the pictures). Although growing up I don't remember having a Christmas, I can say from the few pictures I saw, I had a Christmas before. I don't remember when Christmas stopped, but I know they stopped at the pictures shown to me. As my mother continued to flip through pictures in her huge paper bag, there were more pictures of our family always smiling, laughing, and having fun. Suddenly the pictures of my father and me stopped showing up. I asked my mother what happened after I was three, and she said, "Your daddy loved you, but he couldn't stop living his life." I thought to myself, *I see that runs in the family. I mean that's kind of what you did to me by beating my brains out and causing me to live from foster home to foster home, but we are not gonna talk about that.* Anyway, my mother started to explain my father's actions and how he was in and out of my life. Long story short, my daddy served in the army and had another family that he cared about more.

    I have a few memories with my dad in them, but they weren't good memories at all. The mind is so powerful, yet it is still flawed; it will only let you see one side of someone and not the other sides of that person. I had a different viewpoint about my father from the pictures I observed. There are about four memories I have with my daddy, none of which involve birthday cakes or Christmas trees and certainly not with toys under the tree. I remember a time when I was about nine years old. I hadn't seen my father in a few years when he showed up out of the blue knocking at the front door. At the time, my mother was not home. The rule was: "Don't open my damn door for nobody when I'm not here; I mean nobody or I'm gonna whip your ass." I personally knew this to be true because of the time I opened the door for my brother when my mom wasn't home. Mommy came in while my brother was there, and the first thing she asked was who opened the door. At my confession, Mommy snapped at me, "What did I say about my door when I'm not here?" I explained the rule and my reason for breaking it, which was "because he is my brother." *Ent*, wrong answer. My mom got a broom and whipped me from downstairs all the way to my room. It wasn't the cheap broom with the plastic broom stick either; it was the broom with the wooden broom stick. She whipped me until the broom cracked on me. She threw the part of the broomstick that didn't have the brush at the end at me, striking me in the face before my beating (which I later learned to be abuse) ended. "I told your ass not to open my god damned door for nobody, but you don't listen. Take your ass to bed," my mom yelled. There were welts and bruises and little cuts on my arms and legs. So yeah, I learned my lesson and all of my other sisters who watched learned a lesson, too. Anyway, my father was banging on the door.

My older sister Trina shouted, "Who is it?"

My father answered, "It's your father, open the door."

Even though I haven't seen him since I was three, his voice sounded so familiar. I was so excited to hear his voice and wanted to open the door for him, but I knew I couldn't see him. I answered from behind the door telling him, "Mommy said I can't open the door when she ain't here." He kept saying things like, "I am your dad," and "You have to open the door for me," making me feel guilty, but my flashbacks told me otherwise.

In the living room there was a large window from wall to wall with maybe two inches of wall space on either side of the window. Directly under the window was a long couch about the same width of the window. My dad walked away from the door, walked across the porch over to the window from the outside, and dove through the window. At the sound of the shattered glass falling to the floor, my two younger sisters, my niece, and my nephew started to cry. The window was demolished; there was glass everywhere, all over the couch and living room floor. There was blood dripping from my father's lacerated hands, with the blood blending in with the red carpet on the floor. My dad shook and stomped the glass off as if he was a wet dog shaking water off or something. He sat on the couch with his legs crossed; his right ankle was over his left knee. He sat as if nothing ever happened; he even waved his bloody hands to signal us to come and talk to him. Trina was standing in front of me and my little sisters with her arms straight out from side to side to block us from the glass that was everywhere. I was hugging on my siblings trying to calm them down and telling my dad he can't stay, that he has to leave before Mommy gets home. As much as I wanted to see my dad, I became cognizant of his ways and didn't want to see him in this manner. Even though I didn't let him in, I still felt responsible and afraid to face my mother when she arrived.

Sometimes people or circumstances will make you feel like you are responsible for the things that transpired in your life, but knowing what I know now, I see that I couldn't control others, their beliefs, their actions and the reasons why they inflicted pain onto me. I shouldn't have to have felt responsible; I was just a child. If you are reading this, please know that you were not and never will be responsible for the way people mistreated you. You can't take the blame for someone else's decisions. Free yourself of that responsibility and take responsibility for how you want to live from now on. Take responsibility for the things you can control and pray for the things you can't control.

After the dramatic entrance my father made by plunging through the window, my mom let him stay. It was evident that she didn't want him there, but he said he wasn't leaving, and by the looks of it, my mom wasn't ready to fight for her decision. I think she just wanted the night to be over with no trouble. Well, that night they got into a fight anyway. It was about 10:30ish when I heard rumbling and tumbling along with the sound of my mother screaming while gasping for air. I got out of bed and walked two bedrooms over past the bathroom to see my father choking my mother up against her bedroom wall next to the window. My mother's back was pinned up against the wall with my father's right hand around her neck, his head pressed against the left side of her face. He had his right leg between both of her legs and his left arm pressed against the wall. I was so afraid because I never saw my dad hurt my mom. I'm pretty sure this wasn't the first time, but it was just the first time that I saw it and was old enough to understand what was going on.

My mother's eyes were closed, and then they opened for a quick second. She saw me watching and tried to reach out to me. I thought she was reaching for my help. I ran into my mom's room and grabbed the first thing I saw, which was a lamp on my mom's dresser. The lamp was plugged in and turned on. I snatched that lamp right out of the wall; ran, and jumped, hitting my dad in the back with the lamp. I was aiming for his head, but I had to be only 4 ft tall to his 6 ft 2 inches. My dad kicked me in the stomach without even turning around to see if he hurt me, not loosening his grip from around my mom's neck. *As I write these words on paper, I believe my mom was trying to wave me away because she knew what would happen.* Suddenly, my mother turned somehow and bit my dad on the neck. I guess it was momma bear strength. He loosened his grip that time, holding onto his neck. My mother ran past him coughing, still gasping for air, rushing over to my balled-up body on her cold hardwood floor. She kneeled and hovered over me trying to get me up. "Come on baby," she whispered. I couldn't get up fast enough because of the pain I was going through. My father turned and yelled, "Bitch, you bit me, you fucking bit me!" He started to kick and punch my mother while she was hovering over me. She didn't fight back; she took it all, protecting me from the blows.

The blows didn't last much longer. It was like my dad had snapped out of it and realized what he had done to me. From inside my mother's pouch, I felt the pressure of the blows stop. I heard my father step back away from my mom crying, "No, no, no, no" repeatedly. I imagined he was holding onto his head wondering what happened. My mother was still hovering over me for a few seconds and then lifted herself just enough to fall off of me and roll on the side of me. Although my mother took the blunt of the blows, I was still hurt and terribly scared of my father. My father stormed out of the room, down the stairs and out of the front door for another two years when I saw him last at his funeral.

Sophie was so distraught at the funeral. She was boo-hooing and sobbing for my father. I didn't understand why she was so dramatic. *I mean, I know he dead and all, but he wasn't there for us,* I thought. Instead of comforting her, I started to laugh *not out loud because that would have been rude,* but I held it in. I buried my face into my hands as if I was crying, but I was laughing and crying. *When I get a good laugh, it always brings tears to my eyes.* My family probably thought I was crying for a little bit, but I got myself together quickly. I had to stop looking at Sophie, or I would have busted out laughing from the faces she was making when she was crying.

I was not emotional at all. My mother and other family members thought I wasn't emotional because I was nine years old. They thought I was too young and didn't understand what was happening. However, I understood very well. I knew exactly what was happening; the man who was in the casket was the man who abused my mother for years. He was the man who abandoned me and left me in the hands of someone whom he taught, through experience, to abuse me. The man in that casket was a dead man who was dead way before he died.

Lyfe

Besides being beat up by my mother and being bullied at school, I was being manipulated by Lyfe. Lyfe was only four years older than me, she had beautiful dark skin and was tall and lanky with short hair that would stick up all over her head. She had big beady eyes that were always a little yellowish in color. She had to be about 5'9" by the time she turned 13. This may sound really bleak, but before I knew the true meaning of hate and learned that Jesus wanted me to love everyone, I hated Lyfe. Yes, she was my sister, but I hated everything about her. I hated that she was sick physically and mentally. I hated that she was a manipulator; I hated how she treated me and Fifi. I hated the fear she added to me, and I hated the things she made me do. Every day she bossed Fifi and me around. She trapped us into doing stupid stuff just by telling us, "If you don't do what I say, I'm gonna tell Mommy." Fifi and I were so afraid of Mommy that we literally did anything Lyfe told us to do even when we knew it was wrong. It was part of the lost voice we've had since birth.

Lyfe was addicted to money, smoking, sex, and rebellion, and she was willing to risk it all to get those things.

Lyfe got into lots of trouble; she skipped class, stole from everyone including my mother, she smoked, and was promiscuous at a young age, but didn't get punished much because she had sickle cell anemia. Sickle cell anemia is when the red blood cells in your body become sickle shaped cells. These sickle shaped cells stop the blood flow to your bones, organs and muscles. The insufficient blood flow to these major areas in the body causes mild to severe pain; and in Lyfe's cases, the pain was always severe. Lyfe said it felt like someone was repeatedly beating her with a hammer all over her body. I felt bad for Lyfe whenever she had to go through those crisis moments. Sometimes Lyfe would have crisis moments where she felt like she was about to die from the pain. There were times when we would be sitting at the table eating and *boom*, Lyfe would start screaming and yelling, rolling on the floor, crying in pain. When Lyfe wasn't going through her painful crisis moments, she was up to no good and knew that because of her disease, she could get away with murder.

Although Lyfe didn't get beat as much as I did, there was this one beating that caused Lyfe to go into a crisis moment, which is why my mom didn't want to beat Lyfe anymore (*perhaps my mom did care for us; or maybe she just cared for Lyfe*). She was like 14 years old. Lyfe was skipping class, and my mom received a call home from her teacher; I just knew it was game over for Lyfe. Lyfe came home from school wearing different clothes from the hammy downs (hand-me-downs) my mom sent her to school wearing. Her dingy white yellow sweat suit was replaced with a t-shirt that stopped midway of her belly and shorts that were super high with high white socks, but the same holey no name sneakers from the thrift store on her big feet. My mom was waiting at the door with a belt in her hand. Now I don't wish the worst on anyone, but I never got beat with a belt. A belt is the easiest weapon to get beat with, but somehow Lyfe and Sophie got beat with a belt, while Fifi and I got beat with sticks, 2x4 planks, extension cords, glass, and whatever other deadly weapon you can think of that was laying around. Anyway, I digress. My mom started yelling at Lyfe saying things like, "You stupid hussy, all you do is skip class. You out there being a whore in the school bathrooms with these slutty clothes you got on." Lyfe tried to plead her guilty case, but my mother started swatting away at Lyfe with her belt. Though she only hit Lyfe with the belt about five to six times, she beat her with the buckle part, leaving Lyfe with welts and open cuts on her body. After Lyfe got her beating, my mother cleaned and iced her wounds, apologizing and treating her as if Lyfe never disobeyed her rules. Even though Lyfe was disobedient, my mother didn't want to hurt Lyfe because of her sickness. Later on that night, Lyfe had a crisis moment and had to be sent to the hospital for treatment. I don't remember if the doctors asked my mother what happened to Lyfe with the welts and cuts on her, but I'm sure she made up some great story. Lyfe knew the power of her sickness and used it against us to get what she wanted no matter the cost.

We didn't get a regular allowance or any type of money in our hand for anything from our mother, but Lyfe found a way for us to get money. It started with fighting; Lyfe would make Fifi and I fight with each other. She would take us to the playground at the intersection of 33rd and Diamond Street when my mother wasn't home and make us fight each other in front of her friends. Her friends would bid on who was going to win the fight. Her friends mostly bid on Fifi since it was very cinch for Fifi to play along with Lyfe's games because she liked to fight. For me, I thought it was wrong to make your sisters fight each other in front of your friends and get paid for it. To get the fight started, Lyfe would put a chip on Fifi's shoulder and tell me to knock it off. Lyfe's friends would be shouting and chanting, "Fight, fight, fight" while they pumped their fist in the air circling around us. I just stood there not willing to participate, but then Lyfe would start pushing me toward Fifi so I could bump into her and aggravate her, and it worked every time. Fifi always saw that I didn't want to hit her, but she went on ahead and swung at me anyway. I tried to hold out as much as I could, but once her hits started to hurt, I fought back. While we were fighting, I could hear my sister saying, "Yeah, give me y'all's money, pay up bitches," to her friends. I caught a quick glimpse of them passing their bills around. She was really getting paid to make us fight. Fifi had a very hot temper; when Lyfe broke up the fight, Fifi was furious. It was like she was just getting started; she wanted more because she was upset that I beat her. Lyfe checked Fifi and all of a sudden, she calmed down. Lyfe had this hold over Fifi; another thing I hated about Lyfe, how she could control Fifi the way she did. After all the fighting we did, Lyfe gave us two dollars each while she kept the rest to herself. After a while, Lyfe stopped making Fifi and I fight each other and started having us fight other girls Lyfe had problems with in the streets. Fifi and I became professional fighters in the streets; we worked for Lyfe.

Part of my working for Lyfe was making sure she had whatever she wanted. One time when my mother was out for a few days and left Lyfe in charge, Lyfe wanted something to eat that wasn't in the house. When my mother wasn't home, we weren't able to use the stove, so we had to fend for ourselves with cold and quick foods. We didn't have a microwave, so it was nothing that could be heated up quickly.

We had to eat cereal with water, wish sandwiches (when you wished you had some meat) with just mayonnaise and ketchup on the bread , syrup sandwiches, sugar sandwiches and other quick things of the sort. This one particular day Lyfe wanted something different, so she made us go with her to find food to eat. I didn't understand how we were just going to find food, but Lyfe had a plan.

"We're going to walk until we find some food to eat, and you're going to get the food for me," Lyfe explained to Fifi and me.

I asked "how we were just going to find food.", and she pointed to the trash cans on the corners of the block.

"I ain't digging through no trash cans for nobody," I responded. Lyfe smacked me across my face and said, "You're gonna do what I tell you to do, bitch." Fifi was excited for some reason. "Shit, I'll do it because I'm hungry, too." We walked a few blocks digging in trash cans to find food that wasn't finished that could be eaten. This one trash can we checked was so nasty; it had wet stuff in it and ugh, used condoms, empty chip bags, and you know, trash. We didn't find anything in that trash can. A different trash can we went to had a McDonald's burger still in its wrapping. It looked like it had only been bitten one time, so it was edible. Lyfe took a bite and was chewing like she never ate before, *although we had never had McDonalds before, so I could see her amazement*. She gave Fifi a bite, and she was hyped about it; we never had McDonald's before, so I really wanted to try it. I took a bite, and it was soooo good. It tasted like heaven; the burger had cheese, onions, pickles and ketchup on it, and it was so good. I actually wanted another bite, but Lyfe ate the rest by herself. I guess one bite was our payment for a job well done of digging through trash cans. In that same trash can, Lyfe found a 16ounce Mountain Dew bottle filled with liquid. Now we never had Mountain Dew before, but by the look of the bottle, I knew it was not filled with Mountain Dew. I had been in stores enough to know what Mountain Dew looked like; it looked like a light green water with bubbles in it. This bottle of Mountain Dew had a darker liquid with no bubbles; it looked more like iced tea in the bottle. I put two and two together and knew right away that it was liquid from a boy. It was piss, and I was not going to be a taste tester. I told Lyfe it didn't look like soda, but she didn't listen. Lyfe took the Mountain Dew bottle out of the trash can, opened it, took a big gulp, and spit it out immediately.

"This is piss; this ain't no soda," she said, spitting the soda out onto the ground and wiping her tongue off with her arm. Fifi and I busted out laughing. "I told you that wasn't soda," I said while laughing. After cursing me out for laughing, Lyfe continued searching through trash cans. I was done for the day. I just followed along with Lyfe. Needless to say, Lyfe did not learn her lesson and neither did Fifi and I. On days we were hungry and couldn't cook when my mother wasn't home, we went searching through trash cans.

Lyfe took advantage of the time my mother wasn't home *(and my mother wasn't home much)* to make her money. She would pimp Fifi and me out to the boys on the block and a few other older boys Lyfe knew from around the way. It all started when we snuck out to the playground; it was Lyfe, Fifi, Sophie and me along with the boys on our block Meek, Slim and Rob. I liked Rob because he was quiet like me, and didn't want to get into any trouble, but was too chicken to speak up for himself around his "squad." As soon as my mother left the house, got in her car, drove off and waited about five minutes (because Mommy liked to go around the block sometimes to see if we would sneak out), Lyfe told us to get dressed while she went to the boys' houses to let them know we were going to the park. Once we were all dressed, we walked to the park right up the street from us. We had to stay close so that it would be easy for us to get back home before Mommy got home. Lyfe introduced the game "Catch a Girl, freak a Girl," a twisted game of tag where the boys would chase the girls and hump them a few times and sometimes more. When we reached the park, the boys would yell "run," and we would run all around the park trying not to get caught by the boys. I, especially, was trying not to get caught by Slim; I wanted to get caught by Rob because I thought he would be scared to try anything, and we would just sit and talk. Lyfe got caught by Slim, and they went behind a wall in the park and did whatever; Fifi got caught by Meek and were humping each other like wild rabbits in the open; and I got caught by Rob. Rob looked at me, and I looked at him, then he just grabbed my vagina with his whole hand. I jumped back.

"Ugh, get off of me!" I yelled.

"Well, why you playing? It's a game," he responded back with an attitude walking toward me with a grimacing look on his face, grabbing my vagina again and rubbing his hand back and forth. I was used to being manipulated by my mother, by Lyfe and by the students at school, so I operated in fear. A fear came over me that I once knew from Lyfe and my older brother when they used to touch me in inappropriate places. I looked down while Rob continued to touch me. *It's just a game,* I thought through my manipulated and programmed mind. I joined in the moment, rubbing my hands on his package through his pants until the game was over. I felt like the whore my mother always called me and like I deserved to be treated as such at the early age of 10. We would go on and play that game whenever we had the chance to sneak out and make it to the playground. The boys always caught the same girl; Lyfe got caught by Slim, Fifi got caught by Meek, and I got caught by Rob. Then, it was time to up the ante.

Later, Lyfe ordered the boys to come over to our house one day while my mother was out doing her thing. The boys came to the backyard, and Lyfe had Fifi and me meet them in the yard. In order to get to my backyard, the boys had to walk around the corner and through an alleyway that was about 3 - 4 ft wide. My backyard was a nice size for a few children to go out and play. It was about 16 ft long and 15 ft wide; the ground was split horizontally between tall grass and pavement. The yard was closed in on three sides by 6 ft gates and the house as the fourth side. Slim, Meek, and Rob came through, opened the gate that never had a lock on it and knocked on the back kitchen door waiting for us to come to the door. Lyfe opened the door, and Fifi and I followed behind her, leaving Sophie in the house by herself to greet the boys. "How much y'all got?" Lyfe started the conversation off with one hand on her hip and the other signaling for them to pass their money over. The boys dug in their jean pockets, pulling out a few 1's and 5-dollar bills.

"What you want done?" Lyfe asked the boys while snatching their money out of their hands *as if she was asking about a hairstyle.*

"You know what we want, stop playing!" Slim answered.

"You can get your dick sucked for this, and that's it." Lyfe answered, while counting the money in her hand. Fifi and I looked over at Lyfe like she was crazy; I had no idea what she meant or to whom she was referring. Apparently, this was a conversation Lyfe had with the boys without Fifi's or my knowledge. Lyfe put the money she took from the boys, which added up to be $16, (I counted as she was playing with the money) in her pocket and pushed Fifi and me to the boys and said, "Go suck their dick" so casually like this was no big deal or like we agreed on this prior to this encounter. As soon as the word "dick" came out of Lyfe's mouth, the boys started to unbutton and unzip their jeans, thinking they were going to get lucky.

Now I know I took a lot of crap from my mother *because I felt like I had to* and the people at school *because I was scared of being punished at home,* but I ain't never been no real pushover for my sisters, not even Lyfe. As far as I was concerned, we were all on the same level playing field when it came to fighting and being able to take pain. My mom contributed that to us all, to Fifi and me more than Lyfe and Sophie, but we all knew how to inflict pain and how to take pain. Anyway, I looked at Lyfe with a straight face, boldness in my throat, and said, "I ain't doin' that shit; that shit is nasty!" not caring what the consequence was going to be, knowing full well Lyfe would name her price.

Lyfe screamed, "Bitch, you're gonna do what I tell you to do or I'm gonna tell Mommy you stole her pennies out of the penny jar!"

"You always saying, 'I'm gonna tell Mommy about the same thing. I don't care, tell her; she not going to do nothing but beat me anyway!" I screamed back.

For that was always the price Lyfe used over my head; under normal circumstances, I would do whatever Lyfe blackmailed me to do to avoid getting my behind whipped, but this was a different story. I was not willing to relinquish my dignity in this way, and I didn't. The boys are just looking back and forth at us, waiting impatiently with their pants down to their ankles, showing their colorful boxers.

"We already gave up our money," Slim blurted with an attitude.

"Aight, you gonna get something," Lyfe said, sucking her teeth with an attitude. Well, y'all gonna have to give up some ass or something!" Lyfe said to Fifi and me.

"Yo, I'm tired of the back and forth," Slim said, grabbing onto Lyfe. Meek and Rob followed suit, grabbing Fifi and me. Rob grabbed me and turned me around forcefully against the gate. He then grabbed my hands and lifted them around my head as he pushed his body against my body. I was still fully clothed with my dingy t-shirt and dirty tights. I pushed my butt back toward him yelling, "Don't touch me! Get off of me!" trying to get out of his grip, but Rob was too strong. He fell back a little, but he regained his strength by leaning up against me with one of his forearms and elbow pressed up against my back and pulling my tights and panties down with the other hand at the same time. His elbow was hurting my back, but I knew pain and knew how to fight through it; however, it was hard to fight through the mental pain of what was happening, what was being allowed to happen to me by Lyfe. That was a pain I couldn't fight through in my head.

Rob began to try and put his little soft penis in my vagina; moving back and forth missing the hole because I think this was his first time having "sex" just as it was mine. *Dumb ass, he don't even know what do, even I know it goes in the hole,* I thought still in anger but laughing in my head. I was relaxed and didn't put up much of a fight because I thought he wouldn't be able to get it right anyway, and I would win this new battle I've never experienced before. His penis started to get a little harder when soon enough, he found the hole. It hurt a little once it finally got in, but it wasn't unbearable, perhaps because Rob's penis was still small or maybe I was used to being fondled by my brother's fingers or maybe because I was numb to pain by now. I don't know, but it didn't physically hurt much for it to be my first time. Sidebar: In fact, growing up, I never counted this time as my first time because it didn't hurt the way people talked about their first time being so painful and how they bled afterwards. Those things didn't happen to me, so I discounted the opportunity of it being my first time. While Rob is doing his thing, my fingers are gripped around the chain linked gate, allowing me to push back with some power, but still not strong enough to get Rob off of me.

"Un huh, you thought I wasn't going to get in there, didn't you?" he asked me. The question may as well have been rhetorical because I did not answer. I was still angry and in shock that he actually made it in as he continued to push in and out of me, *this isn't a game anymore; this is sex, sex,* I thought. It was over fairly quickly after all of this white stuff came out of his penis and all over me, dripping down my legs. It was disgusting; I was disgusted; I was a whore, a juvenile prostitute making a whopping two dollars per hit. For the first time, I was finally living up to one of the many nicknames my mother called me. Rob got off of me panting and limping backwards like he had hurt himself or something. I pulled up my panties and my pants, ran past Fifi and Lyfe yelling, "I hate you" at Lyfe. Lyfe yelled back, "You'll get over it." I ran to the bathroom crying, cleaning myself off with a rag, gagging over the sight and the feel of all the white stuff on me. Although I was angry and upset at Lyfe, at the young age of 10, I learned how to celebrate small victories. *At least I didn't suck his dick,* I thought. This behavior went on for the next year, a few times a week as the boys made their way actually inside of our house when my mother was gone. Although I never forgot, Lyfe was right; I did get over it.

Caught

The last time I remember selling my body to Rob, was the day we got caught planning the next sexual appointment. Slim, Meek, and Rob were a part of the lookout when my mother left the house. They were always outside; their parents let them outside as soon as they woke up, it seemed, until it was time for the street lights to go on. They knew what my mom's car looked and sounded like. My mom had a red two door Ford Escort that talked. *Yes, you read it* — the car talked, and it was so cool to me because I had never heard of that before. When I didn't put my seat belt on fast enough, it would say, "Please fasten your safety belt" repeatedly until I fastened my seat belt. When the door wasn't closed all the way, it would say, "The door is ajar" repeatedly until the doors were closed. I never knew what *ajar* meant until I became an adult (don't judge me); I thought, *how could the door be a jar? The door is a door, and a jar is a jar. Somehow, I never noticed that my mom would open and close the doors after the car gave that message.* The car made a very loud screeching noise, so loud it could be heard in the backyard and from anywhere on the block. The car was also a part of the lookout.

We had a system for whenever my mom left the house. First, my mom had to leave the house, of course, because we weren't on a suicide mission. Next, when my mom drove off the block, the boys would wait a few minutes after she was gone. Then, they would walk around the back alleyway to come through the gate to our back door. After that, they would knock on the back door nine times to the same beat of *The Three Little Pigs* when The Big Bad Wolf said, "Little pig, little pig, let-me-in!" Lyfe came up with this system; I had no parts. Finally, Lyfe would collect her money from the boys, and we would get to work doing nasty things no child should have been doing.

One day after my mom left, the boys came knocking on our front door. This was unusual because they knew to come around the backyard and knock on the back door. That was always what we did so no one on the block would see them sneaking in our house. The boys knocked on the front door, but my sisters and I knew we weren't supposed to answer the door. We wanted to know who was at the door so bad. *Well, what if I look through the peephole to see who is at the door? Technically, I didn't have to answer the door; I could just see who was at the door,* I thought. I took it upon myself to follow through with my thoughts. "It's the boys!" I said to Lyfe.

"Go see what they want, but just talk to them through the mail slot," Lyfe instructed, and I listened.

Fifi and I bent down on all fours to the mail slot at the bottom of the door. The mail slot had to be about three inches high from the floor. We opened the mail slot and started to talk to the boys.

"What y'all want?" I asked.

"You?" Rob answered.

"Get out of here," Fifi chimed in.

We started to talk to the boys for about five minutes. They were asking us why they can't come in and talking about all kinds of nasty stuff they wanted to do to us sexually and vice versa. Then, all of the sudden, a different voice appeared behind the boys. It was hard to see the person because of how small and low the mailbox was, and how the three boys were all trying to get facetime in that small space. Although we couldn't see the person, we recognized the voice; it was my mother's voice. No one knew how long she was standing behind the boys. We certainly didn't hear her car coming down the block because we would have broken that meeting up with the quickness.

At the sound of my mother's voice, the boys backed away from the mail slot and tried to get up as quickly as they could. My mother stood 6 feet tall right behind them saying in a calm, but sarcastic voice, "Oh, don't stop now. What else are you going to do to them?" The boys got up, apologizing to my mother and running away quickly. Fifi and I backed up away from the mail slot and ran up the stairs to our rooms as if we weren't talking to the boys at all. *Looking back, I can't believe I thought this would work, my mother was no dummy.* Sometimes when my mom caught us in a lie, she would say, "I may have been born at night, but I wasn't born last night," which was another saying I never understood until I became an adult. My mother opened the door with her key and yelled to us, "Get y'all's slutty asses down here now!" Lyfe, Fifi and I came slowly down the stairs, bunched together on the bottom of the steps, afraid for our lives. Lyfe started babbling off at the mouth. "It was Meena and Fifi! When the boys knocked at the door, Meena ran down and started talking to them. They were talking nasty to each other," she said. If looks could kill, Lyfe would have been dead as soon as I turned my head to look at her annoying face. I was furious because she forgot to mention she told me to ask them what they wanted. My mother grabbed me so fast by the front of my shirt, almost ripping it right off my back; that's how hard she gripped me up. "Strip!" she yelled at me. "And you too!" she yelled at Fifi, never calling Lyfe. I suppose she didn't call Lyfe because Lyfe was not seen or heard in the mail slot, so she didn't get in trouble. I couldn't help but think, *but what about getting in trouble just for not watching us properly?* "Take all of your clothes off. I'm going to show you how to hoe," my mother said angrily yet sarcastically, with her tight lips curled up, and her face twitching. My mother walked through the kitchen and fiddled around in the cabinets. *What is she doing? What is she going to do to us? I thought.* Fifi and I were crying and undressing, and Lyfe was just standing at the bottom of the stairs with that stupid smirk on her face. Sometimes, I swore Lyfe enjoyed seeing us get in trouble; she enjoyed seeing us in pain. I don't ever remember — not once — Lyfe consoling me after a beating or any type of discomfort from anyone. My mother came back into the living room with a bag of cornmeal, a bucket of water, and two scrub brushes. "Y'all want to be hoeing around in these streets, on your knees, and laying on your backs. Put your backs into this." My mom poured out the entire 2 lb bag of yellow cornmeal on the red carpet and threw the empty bag in my face. She slammed the bucket of water on the floor between; water splashed out of the bucket onto the carpet with the cornmeal. The cornmeal started to clump together like wet sand at the beach. "Scrub all this shit up or it's gonna be yo' asses! When I get back, this shit better be cleaned; not nothing better be left," she said, kicking us into the batch of wet cornmeal and walking out of the front door. My bare knees hurt so bad as they were now kneeling on the wet and dry cornmeal on the floor, leaving little gritty prints on my knees; it felt like sandpaper. As soon as the front door slammed closed, Fifi said, "How the fuck we gonna get all this shit cleaned up with a scrub brush and a bucket of water? I hate her, yo." I came up with a plan where we would scoop all of the cornmeal into our hands, put it in the bucket until it's almost gone, and then scrub the rest up. We started to scoop and clean, scoop and brush. We barely used any of the water, as it made the floor messy. The scrub brush only spread cornmeal around to different areas of the carpet, making it harder to clean, which is what I had predicted would happen.

My mother had been gone for about 10 minutes before she came back to the house. Fifi and I were butt naked on the floor on our hands and knees trying to finish up cleaning. We were so afraid because we weren't finished yet, and we knew there would be hell to pay. *How did she get back so fast? How come I didn't hear her car pull on the block?* I thought to myself. My mother came through the front door with her boyfriend, Mr. Matthew, following behind her. Turns out my mother's car broke down around the corner. She couldn't get it to start back up, so she walked back home to call Mr. Matthew on the house phone and asked for help. Mr. Matthew was a mechanic and a lifesaver. When Mr. Matthew came in and saw Fifi's and my malnutritioned, skinny butt naked bodies, he ordered us to go upstairs in his deep, but strained voice. Mr. Matthew had a weird voice because he threw up a lot after he ate. Anyway, Fifi and I looked up at my mother for her approval, and she yelled, "Get yo' asses upstairs." We got up, holding our arms around our skinny imaginary private areas. We left the bucket, the scrub brush, and the rest of the cornmeal right where we stood on that red carpet. As Fifi and I ran up the stairs with our flat backsides showing, I could hear Mr. Matthew telling my mother, "You shouldn't treat them like that; they are just little kids." He never yelled at my mother nor did he ever yell at any of us. Mr. Matthew was a very nice and caring man who really loved my mother and us, just as he loved his own children.

My mother was yelling at him saying, "Those are my children; you don't tell me what to do with *my* children!"

"You're drunk. Sit down and relax. You shouldn't be drinking and driving, anyway," Mr. Matthew said in his non-threatening voice.

My mother did what she was told, and at last, we were saved from that whooping.

The Red Carpet

"Lei'Lynn, get yo' ass in this house right now!" my mom yelled after our neighbor a few doors down, Ms. Neechi, walked into our house. Ms. Neetchi was my mother's drinking partner. She had two children: one girl and one boy. Sometimes my mom and Ms. Neetchi went to the speakeasy together, and they'd both leave their children home unattended for hours or days at a time. Although neither family was allowed to go outside, when our parents went out together, we would sneak out and go to one another's house for a few hours and talk about how we hated our mothers when they were drunk. Ms. Neetchi was way better than my mother because she didn't abuse her kids; she was a functional alcoholic who took care of her kids, but she was very clumsy and loud when she was drunk. Anyway, Ms. Neetchi walked right past the living room, past the dining room where I was cleaning, and straight into the kitchen where my mother stood. She stood right in the doorway between the kitchen and living room excited to tell my mom something. I knew right away Lynn was in trouble when my mom said her whole name. Ms. Neetchi was cracking up when she said, "Listen to your granddaughter; I asked her where you were, and she said, 'In the house somewhere, probably smoking or drinking or something,' with her hands on her hips, standing like this." Ms. Neetchi was standing in a pose with her left leg bent a little and her right hand pushing the right side of her hip to the left with her lips poking out. By the laughter and how Ms. Neetchi explained it, it seemed so cute the way Lynn said it, but my mother didn't take it that way. "Oh, she did now, did she?!" my mom replied. By the end of Ms. Neetchi's news, I was scared for Lynn's life already. Lynn was still sitting on the front porch when my mom yelled for her. She walked into the house yelling, "Yes, Grandma?" in her little six-year-old voice, sounding so innocent, not realizing what was about to happen. My mom walked past Ms. Neetchi in the kitchen, past me at the living room table, and met Lynn at the living room entrance. As soon as she met Lynn, she smacked her clean across her face, yelling, "What did I tell you about your grown ass mouth?" I instantly found a corner and bent down to cover my ears, while Ms. Neetchi immediately stopped all her laughing and smiling and hesitantly let herself out of the house. She walked past me in the corner and then past Mommy and Lynn saying, "Umm, Cordelia, I will be back later," and went straight out the front door. Lynn had fallen backward from the back hand she just received and was lying straight on her back on the red living room floor, crying her eyes out. Mommy straddled her legs so that she was standing right over Lynn, bent over yelling in her face, "What did I tell you about running your got-damn mouth? You are a damn child talking like you're a grown ass woman. I should bust your fucking mouth wide open." I don't think my mother gave it any thought because as soon as my mother finished that last word, she balled up her fist, reached back and punched Lynn straight in the nose. I yelled, "Noooo," and ran over toward Lynn. My mom stood up, turned to me, and punched me straight in my nose. There was blood everywhere. Blood was running from Lynn's nose, who was still lying on the floor silently knocked out. I was still standing bent over a little, holding my nose as blood flowed from my nose and hands onto the floor. My mom yelled at me, "What the fuck are you going to do, hunh? You gonna hit me, bitch?" as she was now focused on me instead of Lynn. Although I didn't want to hog up all the attention, I didn't want Lynn to get hit anymore. My mom elbowed me in the back of my neck while my head was down holding the blood in my hands, causing me to fall straight to the floor, face down less than 6 inches away from Lynn. Mom started kicking me in the side while I was on the floor yelling, "You want to help her; stay your ass down there with her." I stayed down as I was commanded, crying and staring at Lynn, waiting for her to wake up. A few seconds later, Lynn opened her eyes. It took her a minute to understand what happened, but I guess she felt the pain and realized what occurred as she started crying uncontrollably, holding her face, and getting blood all over her hands. I inched my way over to Lynn, trying to grab her and hold her when my mom yelled, "Oh, yo' ass still trying to help, hunh?" She walked over to me and stomped on my back and my arms, and then kicked me in the head once. "Get yo' ass up, and clean this Shit up. That's how you can help," my Mother said, wiping her hands on her clothes and walking back into the kitchen as if nothing ever happened.

I got up and picked Lynn up. "Come on niecey-pooh, let me clean you up. You are okay, stop crying and just hold on to me," I said with a shaky voice trying not to cry as much. Something in me told me I had to be strong for my niece and encourage her, letting her know it was not her fault. When we finally reached the bathroom, I sat Lynn down on the toilet seat while I got a few washcloths to wet and started to clean off her face. Lynn flinched and cried a lot while I was cleaning her up. After each time I wiped Lynn's face, I wiped my face to show Lynn that it was okay and that it will get better soon. There was so much bloody water in the sink from the crimson washcloths I kept rinsing. While I cleaned us up, I sang a song very quietly to Lynn singing, "I love you, you love me, we're a happy family with a great big hug and a kiss from me to you, won't you say you love me too," a famous Barney song Lynn loved to watch. When I finished the song, Lynn said, "I love you too, Aunty" and rested her head on my shoulder.

School

School for the most part was an outlet, but honestly, it was just a safer place to be hurt. I attended Dr. Ethel Allen Elementary School on 32nd & Lehigh Avenue, just two blocks away from my house. I attended from kindergarten to third grade. I remember my 2nd grade teacher, Ms. Looney, who was always so nice to me. She was a small, older black teacher who gave me extra attention. I think she knew that something was going on with me at home, and she often saw me get picked on and get into fights with the other kids at school. I was pretty smart from what I remember but was just always in trouble for fighting. Ms. Looney would let me stay after school sometimes and help her with tasks around the classroom. This was one of the ways, I believed, she tried to help me stay out of trouble. Fifi and I were always in fights starting from a young age; we were just troubled children getting in trouble at home every day.

One of the tasks I helped Ms. Looney with after school was washing the large rectangular black chalkboard, spanning about 12 feet, in the front of the class. At the end of each class, Ms. Looney would give me the board eraser to erase the whole board. When I cleaned the board with the eraser, there was like a chalky residue on the board that had to be cleaned with water. Ms. Looney would get a bucket full of water and a sponge (the old 6-inch, yellow sponges that were shaped like rectangular prisms and had visible holes). She showed me how to dip the sponge into the bucket of water, wring it a little, and then wipe up and down the chalkboard in the same motion across the entire surface. This was so fun and relaxing.

    Sometimes Ms. Looney would let me staple papers up on the bulletin board. She taught me how to do that properly so I didn't hurt myself, although I just had to try and staple my finger. It was so interesting to me that something could just click onto something else, and I wanted to see if it would stick to me as well. It was not a good choice, and it didn't feel good after I did it. I took the stapler when Ms. Looney wasn't looking, and pressed it against my finger. Honestly, I didn't think it would penetrate through my skin, I thought it only did it on bulletin boards, but I was sadly mistaken. I took and pressed that stapler on my index finger and screamed bloody murder. Ms. Looney was across the room when she came running over to me in a panic. "What happened? Are you okay?" she said. I showed her my finger with the staple lodged in my finger, crying not able to get a word out. "Okay, okay, it's okay, we are going to the nurse, and she will help you take it out," Ms. Looney assured me as she held my hand and rubbed my back on our way to the nurse that I was going to be ok. It felt like the longest walk to the nurse, but we finally made it, and she began to dig into my skin to remove the staple. "Sweetie, you have to be careful with these things; I showed you how to use the stapler," Ms. Looney said with concern and pity in her voice. Getting the staple out of my finger had hurt worse than getting it stuck in my finger. I had never received any reprimand in such a calm and caring matter from anyone other than Ms. Looney at that school. To everyone else, I was bad, and they didn't want to deal with me and didn't care what happened to me, but Ms. Looney showed me love. Ms. Looney is the first teacher who inspired me to be a teacher, and I am forever grateful for the time she took with me.

Third grade was a totally different story. My 3rd grade teacher was a tall and heavy white man. Mr. Chatsnew was very strict on the class, especially me. He used to make me go last to get in line for some reason. The class was kind of out of control. Mr. Chatsnew would yell and scream at the class all day, every day. It wasn't just me; it was the other children picking with me and me retaliating. This is when I started to get suspended about 10 times a year. There was a bully named Ramona, who happened to be the smallest student in the class. *Looking back, I realized that Ramona was a little person.* Anyway, Ramona would always tell all the students what to do and even hit them, including me. I couldn't understand how the smallest child in the class could intimidate all of us.

One day I decided I wasn't going to let her scare me anymore. I was tired of being bullied every day, fighting all the time and being the only one getting in trouble. One morning, I was trying to put my jacket and bookbag in my cubby, but

Ramona walked by me and pushed me into my cubby head first. I then got up and turned around and pushed Ramona into her cubby, but I pushed her really hard. She fell into her cubby in the sitting position. (It was funny how I sat her down, lol.) I turned my back on her so quickly with the look of "try something." She didn't try me again. Mr. Chatsnew saw the whole thing, but he didn't react until I pushed Ramona. He walked over to me and slapped me in the back with his large man hands, yelling at me to keep my hands to myself. I was so embarrassed; I shrunk into my cubby for the rest of the day, as if I was home getting beat by my mother. The last school bell rang for the day and school was dismissed. I walked home from school, sulking in embarrassment of being smacked by Mr. Chatsnew. When I got home, my mother noticed my disposition and asked me what happened.

"Girl, what's wrong with you?" my mother asked.

"Mr. Chatsnew smacked me in my back today," I responded with my head facing the floor.

"He did what? What the fuck is he putting his hands on you for?" my mother yelled. My head shot up in surprise, because for once, my mother wasn't fighting me, she was fighting for me.

"Because this girl pushed me, and I pushed her back, but she fell into the cubbies, so he smacked me in my back after I pushed her into her cubby!" I cried, soaking it all in.

This made my mother furious. One thing about my mother is she did not play about her kids. It's one thing for her to whip our asses, but no other adult was allowed to lay a finger on us. "Oh, hell no! Let's go, I'm gonna teach him a lesson!" my mother said in anger as she grabbed my hand and stormed out of the house.

My mother was fussing and cussing the whole two-minute ride to the school. All hell was about to break loose as soon as we opened the school doors. When we reached the school and walked through the school doors, my mother went off.

"Where the fuck is Mr. Chatsnew at?" my mother yelled.

"Ma'am, you can't come in here like that; we will not allow you to see him in this manner," the security guard at the front desk explained calmly.

"I'm sorry, my daughter said he smacked her on her back! He should not be putting his hands on my child, or any child that ain't his!" my mother said sternly, waving one hand around while the other rested on her hip.

"I understand that, ma'am. You are absolutely right. Please give me your information so that we can further investigate this matter for you," said the security guard politely.

The security guard called for the prinicipal, Principal Kathy, to help with the issue. Principal Kathy greeted my mother and asked her how she could help. My mother retold the story, and I had to give a formal statement about the incident. Principal Kathy was very familiar with my family and normally didn't care for us because of all the trouble Fifi and I caused, but she seemed to be concerned about the issue at hand.

"I will report this, and an investigation will be started. Once the investigation starts, Mr. Chatsnew will not be able to work until the investigation is over," Principal Kathy explained.

"Thank you because I don't ..." she stopped mid-sentence.

As my mother was talking to the Principal, Mr. Chatsnew came down the stairs, walking down the hallway towards the front door where our impromptu meeting was happening. When I saw him, I clung to my mother, hugging her around her waist.

"There he go right there! You thought I wasn't gonna catch your ass, didn't you? How many other kids are you slapping on?" my mother yelled trying to push past Principal Kathy and the security guard. Both Principal Kathy and the security guard were holding my mother back.

"I don't know what you're talking about. I did not smack your daughter. She is lying!" Ms. Chatsnew declared.

"My daughter would not lie about this. You did, and you're lucky I can't get my hands on you!" my mother responded as the security guard and principal escorted us out of the school. As promised, Principal Kathy reported the incident and DHS implemented an investigation against Mr. Chatsnew. One of the investigators took statements from the other students in the classroom, some parents, and other teachers in the school. Mr. Chatsnew was found guilty at the conclusion of the investigation. I never saw Mr. Chatsnew at school again.

The school had a majority of white teachers, teaching predominantly black children, so that was a struggle for me before I knew it was a struggle. The students were all products of their environment, which meant struggle, survival, and fighting. Leaving the house every morning to go to school was a breath of fresh air. It was a time that I could escape the dangers of living in a home with so many people and an irate, alcoholic mother. It was a time of thoughts about life: what it would be like if my mother was a different person, what it would be like if I were not created, and sometimes, what it would be like if I were to suddenly die. The thought of having to go back home after school was soul-crushing. Before I even reached the school doors, I was thinking about the return home and my safety, only to reach a different type of adversity when I walked through the school doors dealing with teachers who didn't understand me and children who were pure bullies. Eventually, before my third year ended, Fifi and I got expelled from Ethel Allen because of the continuous suspensions.

Fifi and I were transferred to E. W. Rhodes Elementary School at 29th & Clearfield Street, which was a block and a half up the street from my house. When I entered the school premises with my sister Fifi, we were met with bullies. Same issues, different school. As we walked by different groups of people, they would stare, point, and laugh at us. They talked about our clothes, our hair, and the shoes we wore on our feet. They didn't know that Fifi was a firecracker until she blew up. "What the fuck are y'all looking at? If it's a problem, let me know, so I can solve it for you," Fifi blurted as we walked by so many people. Although there was always pent-up anger in my heart from the abuse I endured at home, somehow, I never let it show, even when people deserved my wrath. Fifi, on the other hand, did not give a nothing; she was always over everything and wasn't afraid to show her anger at school. She sho'nuff (sure enough) couldn't show it at home. I was in fifth grade, and Fifi was a grade below me. Fifi and I would separate and go to our different classes once we got into the building, and the same thing would happen each day. As a result of the bullying that took place, Fifi and I always got into fights. We got suspended very often, almost like every two weeks.

Sometimes, on my way to my classroom, I would walk by people and they would put their foot out to trip me. Some people would walk by me and call me ugly and frown at me. Some people actually hit me or pushed me while passing by me. I couldn't understand what made people treat me this way, but I continued to ignore the signs of bullying. There was a bully in my class named Bridget, but she went by "B." She was taller and thicker than me, and she always bossed me around. B would make me carry her books and get her lunch, and then she would send me back to my table. This one particular day, I decided I wasn't going to do that anymore. I was so afraid of this girl in real life, but this day, I had to stick up for myself.

"Ugly, carry my books to class!" she said as she handed me her books.

I slapped all her books out of her hand and onto the floor, saying, "I'm not doing shit!" She was so mad.

"Oh, yeah!" she said looking at her friends, getting ready to prove a point.

"Yeah, Brid-get, go ask one of your little girl friends to carry your books!" I said confidently, exposing her real name to everyone in a taunting tone. Everyone started laughing, putting their hands over their face in awe that I even said anything. B pushed me against the hallway lockers and punched them really hard, scaring me. I didn't move, nor did I hit her. B punched me in my stomach, and then all of a sudden, a rush of anger fell over me. After I recovered from the blow to the stomach, I got up and whaled on B. I bum-rushed her; I bent my head forward, ran straight head first into her stomach, knocking her to the floor. I stood over Bridget and started punching and kicking her all over her body. I felt like I blacked out. We fought for about a minute before one of the teachers broke us up. I fought back, which was something that was foreign to me. I was proud of myself; as far as I was concerned, I won the fight. Because I won, I got suspended for that fight, but not Bridget. For some reason, back in the day when there was a fight between two people, the one who won or came out with the least amount of bruises, was the one who got in trouble.

My 5th grade teacher, Mrs. Witherworth, never said anything to me in school. She never greeted me as if my dirty would rub off on her, and she would give me this disgusting look every time I saw her. This discouraged me from speaking out against my bullies. It wasn't like she was going to help someone she hated. Mrs. Witherworth never told me she hated me, but her actions showed me she hated me. *At least that was the vibe I picked up as a 11-year-old child.* Looking back, I wished I would have told Mrs. Witherworth what was going on with me at home and at school. Maybe she could have helped me along the way if she knew what I was experiencing. Maybe if she knew that I contemplated throwing myself in traffic every day before and after school, she would help. I think I just didn't want to be disappointed if she wouldn't have helped me.

Recess at school was like the Devil's playground. I mean, there were always fights, and Fifi and I were almost always a part of those fights. Fifi and I had the same lunch and recess period, so we would meet up then. No one wanted to sit with us at lunch, so we sat by ourselves. The thing is,

Fifi always had an issue with someone in her class or someone at lunch/recess. She would always come to the table and tell me who she was going to fight. I tried to talk her down, but there is no talking Fifi down. It got so bad that the lunch aides would try to separate us during lunch to avoid any trouble, but we always made our way to each other. We were all we had at that school.

"I'm about to whip this girl ass real quick. Just watch out to make sure her sister or friends don't jump in it," Fifi would say.

"Girl, you always tryna fight somebody," I would reply.

Fifi responded, "Stop bitchin', and be ready to fight. What, you scared?"

"No, I ain't scared! I just don't want to get in trouble when we get home. You know Mommy don't play that!" I said, half scared to fight the girl at school, but more scared of fighting with my mother at home. As soon as we went outside for recess, Fifi spotted the girl she wanted to fight, Tamika. She just walked up to Tamika and started punching her. A crowd started to gather, and I broke the fight up before the lunch aides could get to us. I grabbed Fifi, and we started running around the playground like we were playing tag or something. At that moment, I felt like I had to make an executive decision to break the fight up right away so we wouldn't get caught, and it worked. By the time the lunch aide came over, the crowd had dispersed. We were in the clear, but Tamika was furious.

Lunch and recess were over, and Fifi and I went back to our separate classrooms for the rest of the day. As Fifi and I were leaving school, Tamika and her sister Tamara started walking behind us, telling us they wanted to fight. Fifi turned around ready to go to blows, but I told her no because I didn't want to get suspended. For once, Fifi listened to me, and she turned back around to continue walking home. However, Tamika and Tamara didn't take no for an answer. They followed us, saying things like, "What, you scared? Turn around and fight us, uglies!" I didn't respond to anything they said, but Fifi said things like, "Your mom, you don't want none of this." I turned around once and saw there were so many kids behind Tamika and Tamara following us home. The kids were egging them on yelling, "Fight, fight, fight," "they scared," and a combination of other mean things. Fifi and I just kept walking. We were only about a block away from the house when other kids started throwing things at Fifi and me, like plastic bottles, rocks, and other stupid stuff, but we just kept walking.

We finally made it to our block, and there were more kids than the last time I had looked. It looked like the whole school was behind us, waiting for us to fight. Fifi and I got to our house and knocked on the door. My mother opened the door and asked, "Why are all these kids here on the block like this?"

I told my mom, "The two girls wanted to fight Fifi and me, but we didn't want to fight and get in trouble."

"Well, they are here now, so you may as well fight them!"

I could not believe my ears, so I asked my mother, "So we can fight them?" with a puzzled look on my face.

"Yeah, and you better whip they ass, or I'mma whip yo' ass!"

Without looking back, Fifi and I dropped our bookbags on the porch, pushed past all the kids on the sidewalk, and ran into the middle of the street. This was one of the most amazing times I have ever had on my block. I could hear the kids who lived on my block running up to us saying, "Hold, up, hold up." Almost every kid on the block who was our age ran up to us, including Slim, Rob, and Meek. They all pushed the crowd back to make sure no one was going to jump in our fights. Slim gave us pep talks like, "Yo, whip they ass. I got you; ain't nobody gonna jump in it." *That's one thing I loved about my block, they was hood, and they would ride for anyone who belonged to them. For the first time, I felt like I belonged to something — The Block.* By this time, Fifi and I were in the middle of the street with Tamika and Tamara. The school was behind them, and the block was behind Fifi and me. Slim said, "Fight!" and Fifi and I took the first swing. I swung on Tamika, and Fifi swung on Tamara. There were two fights going on, and all I could hear was the chanting of the school kids, and the chants of the neighbors from my block.

We were going blow for blow, and no one jumped in the fight. I felt so empowered by my mother's encouragement and the block's support that I knew I had to win this fight. I punched, kicked, and even pent Tamika up against a car and was just giving it to her, punch after punch. As Fifi and I were winning the fight, the boys had to break it up because they heard cops coming. Slim grabbed me, while Rob grabbed Fifi, and they rushed us to the top of our porch steps. My mother made us go in the house. Everyone on the block went into their houses and let the school kids disperse on their own. By the time the police got on the block, there were just kids running away in all different directions to get back home. No one wanted to get caught by the police. The one thing everyone had in common, even Tamika and Tamara, was knowing that "snitches get stitches," a unspoken but spoken rule in the hood. When we got in the house, my mother said, "Oh, so y'all be fighting, fighting at school, hunh? I guess I taught you that," as she balled up her fist, blew her breath on her fist, and rubbed her chest and smiled, to take the credit of our victory.

    The very next day at school, Fifi and I got into a fight with some other girls. Tamika and Tamara weren't fooling with us; I supposed they learned their lesson. We actually got expelled from E. W. Rhodes that day because we kept getting suspended for fighting, until they just kicked us out. Just like that, we were expelled again. My mother had to come up to the school and take us home. That was another battle at home we had to enlist in because this was the second school Fifi and I got expelled from, and my mother had to find us, yet again, another school to attend.

The Privileged Girl

I heard keys rattling when my mother opened the front door, so I ran to the top of the stairs. Behind her was a tall, light skinned, pretty girl with long, freshly pressed hair and two travel suitcases. The girl was crying, more like sobbing. "Girl, get on in here, and shut up that noise!" my mother shouted to this girl, as she grabbed her by the hand, pulling her in the house. The girl had a frown on her face and snot running from her nose. Although I wasn't quite sure why the girl was crying, I knew that any kid would be crying if they were with my mother for any amount of time.

I was so curious as to why my mother would bring home a girl with suitcases, but I dare not ask any questions, or it would be me crying and sobbing, but instead with blood coming out of my nose. Instead, I chose to just observe (stare) at the girl and think of how pretty she was, even with her face beet red from crying. Her hair was brown and hanging down the middle of her back. *Wow, look at all the nice, long combed hair she has,* I thought. She had on very nice clothes and shoes that looked new. They looked like they were always her clothes, like she was the only owner of them. *I bet she didn't get them from the hammy downs store,* I thought. The girl's sneakers were name brand and clean, but you could tell she wore them a few times. She had a pair of all white high-top Keds, a pair of sneakers I've always wished I could get from another owner. *Maybe she could hand those down to me when she doesn't want them anymore,* I thought. Even this girl's suitcase was nice. I'm pretty sure it was some kind of designer suitcase of some famous person I didn't know about because they had zippers, buttons, and handles with wheels on the bottom. I had never seen such a cool suitcase before; I don't think I had ever seen a suitcase before. I never moved or went on vacation or anything, so I guess there was really no need for a suitcase. This girl was privileged, but I couldn't help to think about why my mother came home with this privileged girl that I had never seen before. I started to ask and answer all of my own questions in my head like, *is she babysitting? No, she doesn't watch other people's kids, she hardly watches her own kids. Was she trying to teach us a lesson on how if we act right, then maybe we could get nice things like her? No, because no matter what we did, she wasn't going to buy us nothing nice. Is this her job or something? No, Mommy don't work.* It took a lot of brain power to have a serious conversation with myself like this one, but I still didn't come up with anything that made sense. "Listen now, you ain't gone be doing all this crying for nothing, because I can give you something to cry for!" my mother said to the privileged girl. The girl had this frightened look on her face like she had never been beaten before.

"I just want to go home," the girl said, trying to stop crying while trying to catch her breath.

"This is your home now; I don't know why they didn't tell you about me, anyway," my mom said with the attitude of feeling disrespected.

My mother called everyone else downstairs so she could introduce the privileged girl. "This is your sister, Isabella," my mother said so casually, as if it was normal to get a teenager straight out of the womb. Everyone said hi to Isabella with puzzled looks on our faces. *She even has a privileged name,* I thought, *but she is my sister so maybe I'll stop labeling her as privileged because face it, it is not a privilege to be part of this family,* I continued to think. I actually felt sorry for Isabella, for having to join this chaotic arena. "Tameena, take your sister to her room; she is going to sleep in the room with Lyfe," my mother said to me, pointing to the stairs. I did as I was told, and I helped Isabella carry her bags up the stairs to her room. When we reached the room, Isabella looked around the room and saw nothing but bunk beds and dressers. "No closet, no vanity set," Isabella said in disappointment. "No!" I replied feeling equally disappointed and curious as to what a vanity set was. *Don't judge me; I know what it is now.* She started to open her suitcases but then realized there was no dresser space for her to place her things, so she just kept her clothes in her suitcases. I could see some of her clothes when she opened her suitcases a little, and they were nice, clean looking clothes, *better looking than our clothes.*

  Before I could finish my thought about Isabella's clothes and how nice they were, my mother came into the room and told Isabella to take her suitcases back downstairs. She looked at me as if there was hope that she was going back to her old parents, but she was terribly mistaken. My mother took my sister's suitcases and put them in her car and said, "I am going to get you some new clothes; you don't need these anymore," with a weird smirk on her face as she left the house without Isabella.

Eager to know the truth, I blurted out, "Are you really our sister?"

She responded, "Apparently so. I did not know that I had a different mother. No one told me that my mom wasn't my real mom until today."

I felt super bad and tried to make sense of what she just said to me.

"You mean to tell me the person you just left isn't your mom? How did you live with her then?" I asked, needing clarity.

"Your mother birthed me, but I was taken away from her at birth and given to my mom, my fake mom, because your mom wasn't in a good position to take care of me at the time. Today, the people (DHS) came to my house, my fake house, to take me away from my fake mom to take me to my real mom," Isabella explained with tears in her eyes.

I couldn't imagine the hurt she was feeling, but at least she was able to experience a different mother. As we sat on the bottom bunk of the bed, I put one arm around Isabella's shoulder and told her, "It's going to be ok," *lying straight through my teeth,* but she needed to be comforted, so that's what I did — I comforted. I thought it would help cheer her up a little. What I was really thinking was, *poor girl, you about to be on lockdown.* Isabella went on to talk about how she felt hurt for not knowing the truth about her own life, our mother and her fake mother. How all of the sudden she would have to live life without her fake siblings. It seemed like she had a great life before us, and all that was about to change for the worst. To make Isabella feel better, I told her the story of how I always wondered if my mother was my real mother. This one time, I snuck out of the house along with my other siblings, and we walked to the graveyard around the corner from our house. As soon as we walked through the graveyard gate, we saw a tombstone with my mother's full name on it, but it was her maiden name. It read: "In Loving Memory of Cordelia Anne James." We all looked and became so worried about the person we lived with, wondering if she was our real mother. We never investigated any further than the tomb stone, as we shouldn't have been there in the first place.

Shortly after my story was over, my mother walked in the house with a few outfits from the thrift store and beer. She sold Isabella's good clothes for hammy downs. *I still can't believe she would do something so hateful.* She threw a brown paper bag of hammy downs to Isabella for her to see. The clothes were horrible; there were shirts, pants, and shorts, but no matching outfits. "What happened to my clothes and my suitcases?" Isabella said, crying. "What the fuck you just say to me, little girl?" my mother responded as she leapt over to smack Isabella in her face. Isabella didn't know you couldn't ask my mother questions because she saw it as disrespect. Isabella held her face in her hand, crying. "I said I got you some clothes, didn't I? Be grateful for what you have," my mother scolded. Days went by, and Isabella didn't know how to keep up with her nice, long hair. My mother decided to grab a pair of scissors and cut Isabella's hair to about the top of her neck. I stood there in shock while Isabella cried her behind off, as she watched about 10-12 inches of her hair fall to the floor. It was so sad. My mother would often tell Isabella that she thought she was better than the rest of us because of her fancy clothes and her nice hair. I wished I had her life before this happened. That had to be one of the worst days of Isabella's life.

Isabella quickly became accustomed to life in her new home. She learned the "yes ma'ams" and the "no ma'ams," and how to keep up with her chores. Isabella also learned the famous saying: "What happens in this house, stays in this house." She learned not to go telling anybody at school that she got beatings or that she was hungry. For some reason, Isabella didn't get beat as much as Fifi and me. *Hell, no one got beat as much as Fifi and me.* Isabella became my favorite sister during the time she actually lived at our house. She was very nice, polite, and helpful. Sometimes she would help me with my homework, and she would sneak me snacks she got from school. Now, don't get me wrong, Isabella snuck around like I did, but in a more teenage way. She had a boyfriend whom my mother did not know about when she turned 15. I mean, they were really together. Her boyfriend would come over the house when my mother wasn't home, and he would even stay the night. Isabella learned how my mother liked to go out and not return for days at a time, so she took advantage just like us. The name of her boyfriend was "Bam Bam." That's right, a teenage boy they called "Bam Bam." I used to laugh every time I heard his name. Bam Bam was 18 messing around with Isabella. He was rough looking; he had nappy hair and facial hair that wasn't tamed at all. Bam Bam wore his pants down his butt, barely able to walk around properly. I still don't see what Isabella saw in him; even the way he treated her was inappropriate.

    He used to beat on her; she would come home with bruises, crying, and in a bad mood. I didn't realize this was happening, until one day he was at our house in Isabella's room. Fifi, Sophie, and I were downstairs watching TV, which was against the law of the house, when we heard commotion in the room. They were yelling and screaming at each other, and then there was a *pap* sound. He had punched her in her face. "You hit me... You said you wouldn't hit me anymore," Isabella cried. Once I realized what was happening, being the *young feisty, beat everyone but your momma* kind of girl, I grabbed the bat my mother kept by the front door. I headed up the stairs to her room, opened the door, and started swinging on Bam Bam with the bat. Isabella was sitting in the corner with her head in her hand and hand on her knees. She was yelling at me, "Stop, stop Meena," and she grabbed me and the bat. *What is up with these girls in this family letting boys beat on them and blaming me for protecting them,* I thought and still think. Meanwhile, Bam Bam ran out of the room, down the stairs and straight out the front door, calling me a "crazy bitch." Now that I think about it, it was crazy of me to attack him like that because he could have knocked the crap out of me, but I wasn't thinking about that at that time. I just wanted to protect my favorite sister. Not too long after, Isabella left the house behind him, trying to find him to apologize. Eventually, she found him, they made up, and he continued to beat on her, until Isabella ran away from home a few months later.

Isabella could not handle living there with my mother. Oftentimes, she would say how she wished she could find a place to live and take me with her, so I didn't have to live like a mini-Cinderella. She got tired of being hungry, wearing outdated clothes, and watching me get beat; one day while my mother was gone, she packed her bags and left. She did say goodbye, and told my sisters and I how sorry she was for leaving the way she left us (alone). I never cried as hard as I did when my sister left me; it didn't even compare to getting a beating. Isabella took almost everything she had, but left an army green sheet that I kept for keepsake. The green sheet was the only thing I had left to hold on to that reminded me of Isabella. It became like a pacifier to a newborn, or like a thumb to a toddler to me, except instead of sucking my thumb, I sucked my tongue. The green sheet became part of me consoling myself. I would hold a part of the sheet over my face and nose with one hand, while sucking my tongue, and feeling the grooves of the rest of the sheet with the other hand. It had a smell to it that I couldn't resist; I didn't wash the sheet much because it didn't smell good freshly washed. It's pretty weird, but this sheet helped me to sleep at night; it comforted me after beatings and whenever I was overwhelmed. I literally took this sheet wherever I went, and it became a part of my life until I was 35 years old. *Please don't judge me, I've been through some stuff.* Anyway, Isabella ran away, and I didn't see her again for 15 years.

All in all, my sister Isabella was not a privileged girl; she was a young girl who got caught up in the system before she was able to recognize her own mother. There are many other children like her who suffered the same ignorance in discovering who their biological parents were, and I am sure there are more who will discover as time passes. To all the children out there who have shared this same experience, I want you to know that you are not alone. As much damage as this may have caused in your life, you still belong here. No matter who your biological parents are and who is taking care of you, or who has taken care of you, you can still rise above all of the hurt and hardship and become the best person you can be for yourself. I know it sounds easier said than done; so, I challenge you to be the change you want to see happen in your life.

The New School

After being expelled from two other Philadelphia schools, my mother enrolled Fifi and me at Vaux Middle School on 23rd & Master Street, which is now called Vaux Big Picture High School. The school was about a two mile walk from my house on 30th Street. Fifi and I walked two miles to school and two miles back home from school every day. At that time, school tokens were not given out to students for free, the way they are now. My mother couldn't afford to purchase school tokens for the both of us to catch the bus to school, so we walked. Perhaps that is what we deserved for getting expelled from two schools. I wasn't thrilled with the thought of being the new dirty kid at the new school, as that just meant new people to not get along with. However, it turned out that this school was a little different from our other schools.

We didn't get into much trouble, but we also weren't completely away from trouble. I can recall one fight at the new school a friend who was teasing a handicapped girl. (It really wasn't a fight; I beat her up and later we became cool again.)

There was one thing I did not tolerate, which was kids picking on kids with disabilities. My sister Sophie was disabled, and I would do anything to protect her from negative and thoughtless people. For some reason, I felt the need to do the same for that girl in the lunchroom whom I didn't even know. Anyway, I had met a few girls who knew how to sing, and I would normally listen to them while I pretended to do something else so they wouldn't think I was weird. One day at lunch, I was sitting alone and a group of girls came to sit at the same table with their trays of food. I was a little uncomfortable with how close they were; they actually sat at the same table with me. The girls sat on both sides of me and across from me. We hadn't even spoken before; they weren't even in my classes, so I definitely didn't know their names. The girls started talking about music and began singing while they ate. I just sat there listening, but not showing interest, when one of the girls asked me if I knew how to sing, and if I knew the songs they were singing. My head shot up, and I answered, "Oh me, um yeah, you're singing 'G.H.E.T.T.O.U.T.' by Changing Faces," returning my head back down to my lunch tray. "Well, ain't you going to sing something?" one of the girls said. I was so nervous because I had never sung in front of people; I didn't even know if my voice sounded good. It wasn't like I could just walk around my chaotic house singing *la-la-la-las* all willy nilly, like I was in a happy home. I told the girls, "I don't sing in front of people." They replied, "Girl please, just sing." They stared at me intently, waiting for me to start singing, so I did, I started to sing. To my surprise and theirs, I had a voice. It was a little shaky because of the nervousness, but it sounded good. I think it was the first time I heard myself sing aloud in a long time, as it only happened every once in a blue moon when my mother was a happy drunk. "Okay girl, you sound good; you can sing," they explained as they gave me fist pounds and handshakes, to which I did not know how to react. I was in shock. For the first time in my life, I felt good about myself. But then negative thoughts crept in: *maybe I am good at singing, or are they just messing with me.* The journey of my self-worthlessness began. It was then that I began to constantly think about what others thought of me. Even if they seemingly thought fond of me, I would talk myself down. *Am I good at anything?* I thought. I could remember the times when Mommy called me "hussy," "bitch," "stupid," and "dumb ass," none of which felt good. I felt myself battling between my truth and others' perceptions of me. Both concerning in my eyes and hard to grasp at the age of 12.

I don't know what happened because next thing I knew, I was singing with the girls every day at lunch. We never actually sang at talent shows or anything because the school didn't provide after school activities (at least none that I knew of, anyway). Although if they had, I'm pretty sure I wouldn't have been able to participate anyway. My mother made sure I knew to come straight home after school. The streets were not safe for young children, especially young girls. I walked a long way to get to and from school; I didn't have time for anything extra. Even though I was unsure of myself, I still sang with the girls at lunchtime, allowing us to grow closer.

It all seemed too good to be true the way things were going at school. I began to meet more friends, but with more friends came some frenemies. Fifi became popular because of her temper, as I became known for being the sister of a popular girl who had a temper. Then the old school setting started to kick in; the cycle returned and began to spin out of control.

Our first altercation happened between two best friends, Miranda and Tanesha. After a while, Miranda and Tanesha would see us walking around the school or at recess and say things like, "Those new girls stank," and the other girls in their crew would laugh and point fingers. I just thought, *Oh, here we go!* Then Fifi started going off with her trash talking. Miranda walked by Fifi and bumped her shoulder, but before Fifi could react. I grabbed Fifi's hand and said, "Remember, this school year is going to be different." Fifi broke away from me and yelled, "You lucky my sister holding me back, and your mom stank!" as she put up her middle finger and ended the argument.

Fifi and I were walking through the projects to get home one day. Normally, we don't walk through the projects, but for some reason, this day we did. As we were walking through the various buildings of the projects, I saw a few girls about

50 feet away, peeking behind one of the buildings. I couldn't see exactly who it was, but I just had a gut feeling that something was about to happen.

I asked Fifi, "Did you see that group of girls peeking around the corner up there?"

"No, but if they want to fight, we can fight," Fifi responded. We just kept walking, and Fifi was ahead of me. When she turned the corner, a few girls just started whaling on her. I stopped in shock before a few girls started whaling on me. Fifi and I were on the ground getting punched and kicked (beat up) by five girls on us both. It was Miranda's crew and Tanesha's crew who jumped us. Fifi and I held our own for the most part, but we did get beat up. I don't even know who broke the fight up, but the fight didn't last long. My head was killing me from all the kicking those girls did, and Fifi had a bloody nose.

Fifi and I started to walk home, nursing our wounds and fixing our hair so we didn't look like we were in a fight because we didn't want my mother to find out. Both Fifi and I were trying to turn over a new leaf, and not get into too much trouble, which we did, but again, trouble always found us. As we walked home angry and hurt, Fifi started venting and ranting on and on about how we were going to get them back. I just wanted to get home, but Fifi continued in planning her "revenge."

Revenge

Fifi and I planned out when we were going to attack the two best friends who helped jump us in the projects. Well, really Fifi planned the whole thing; I just went along with it. We had to be strategic about it because the girls were not in any of our classes. We had the same lunch period, though, so our option was to either get them early before class or during lunch. We chose lunch, but our plans changed as soon as Fifi saw the girls around 8:30 after our morning meeting in the auditorium. It was time for us to go to our classes. We started to walk up the stairway, and we saw the best friends at the top of the stairs. Miranda and Tanesha came prancing up the steps. There were still other kids walking to their classrooms when Fifi threw the first punch. I was so confused because this was not part of the plan; we said we were going to attack at lunch. *This girl never follows the plan.* I guess seeing the girls so close was too much for Fifi to handle; she just had to attack, and I just followed up.

There were no words spoken. Miranda came up the steps and through the double doors first, then Tanesha followed right behind her. Fifi socked Miranda, I socked Tanesha, and we just started brawling. Kids who were in the halls stopped walking to their classrooms, and kids who were still coming up the steps started to run up the steps to see the fight. As we fought, we moved all around the floor. We were going at it; I was punching, kicking, and kneeing her in the body. Then, Tanesha and I somehow made it into the girls' bathroom. Shortly thereafter, Fifi and Miranda made it in the bathroom, as well. *I still believe the crowd was pushing us into the bathrooms.* It was really tight in the bathrooms; there was about a 2 ft distance between the stalls on the left and the sinks and mirrors on the right. While we fought and many people came to watch, Fifi yelled out, "Put her fucking head in the toilet," so I busted through one of the stalls and did as I was told. Fifi was putting Miranda's head in the toilet, too. It was pretty disgusting, but in that moment, it was what we had to do to show them who was boss. After I put Tanesha's head in the toilet, I kicked her and left her in the stall, brushing past all the kids in the bathroom door. I thought I heard the toilet flush before Fifi came out of the bathroom, so I'm sure she flushed the toilet while Miranda's head was in it, but I didn't know for sure. We ran out of the bathroom and went to class. Surprisingly, no teachers came out to assist or to see what was happening. Fifi and I went straight to our respective classes after giving each other a hug and hand slaps, hoping our sins would not catch up with us.

What happens in the dark, definitely comes to the light. I went to class, and less than five minutes after being there, the principal came in with Fifi. She didn't say a word; she just signaled me with her finger in the "get over here" motion. I sank my head in my desk for a quick second, knowing the problem. My sins had caught up with me, and I knew I was in big trouble, but I didn't know the extent of the consequences I faced. I surely did not expect what came next.

Principal Leinhouser, aka Principal L, grabbed Fifi and me by the back of our shirts and walked us to her office. After we walked in, she slammed the door and gave it to us.

"Do you have any idea how much trouble you're in?" she said in a loud, stern voice.

"Yes, ma'am," I whispered.

"They jumped us first, the other day after school!" Fifi yelled, with her hands in the air.

"SO, YOU PUT THEIR HEADS IN THE TOILET?! I have called your mother, and she is on her way to keep you home for two weeks!" Principal L yelled. "This behavior is unacceptable and will not be tolerated at my school!" she said harshly.

I broke down crying because I knew it was going to be on and popping once we got home with my mother. *We had done it this time,* I thought. Still, I couldn't understand how I was being bullied all school year by multiple people, and I was the one who got caught and suspended for two whole weeks.

When my mother arrived at the school and met us in the principal's office, I started to cry even more hysterically. With a nonchalant voice, my mother grabbed me and said, "Don't cry now; you wasn't crying when you put that girl head in the toilet. I'mma show you when we get home." She fussed at us the whole ride home. "I must send y'all to school to show y'all ass, hunh. Don't worry, I'mma see yo' ass as soon as we get through dem doors. Soon as you get in, strip," she said with her tight lip. Whenever my mother said "strip," it was going to be a nightmare. The car drove up to the house, and I got out of the car and started to walk inside. Before I could get through the door, I was already being attacked. My mother hit me upside the head, knocking me down to the floor, and then kicked me in the house the rest of the way. She reminded Fifi and I to strip while she went to get her extension cord. I started taking off my clothes hesitantly, crying and sobbing as if she would have mercy on me. "Shut up all that noise! You wanted to show yo ass at school, now show yo' ass to me!" my mother yelled. My mother took the extension cord right out the socket, grabbed both ends and put them together, holding them in her dominant hand. This particular beating, she made Fifi and me line up to get beat. To me, it was torture having to watch someone get beat, knowing I was next in line. My mother started to swing at Fifi, and I simply had to close my eyes. Then it was my turn, and she repeatedly swung at me all over my body. I screamed the whole entire beating, which felt like five whole minutes. I was so sore and had welts all over me, except for on my face, although they were really close around my upper neck. It hurt so bad, and began to feel worse after she ordered me to take a bath. The most painful thing to do was get in a tub of hot water with fresh welts all over my body, but I did as I was told.

Fifi and I endured so much during those two weeks of suspension, as we were on a two-week punishment. Punishment consisted of cleaning and beatings all day. If we didn't look like we were cleaning, she would just start beating us with whatever was around at the time. One time she beat me with a baluster (the wooden leg of a banister). She only hit me a few times with it, but it was super painful. Those were the worst two weeks of my life.

China Plates

In the dining room was a tall cherry wood and glass China cabinet, and it was my mom's favorite. That may have been the only thing she herself cleaned. We weren't allowed to touch her China cabinet, but were able to see clearly through it; it was kind of cool. It had about five or six glass rows upon which the dishes and glasses sat. My mom filled it with nice glasses, porcelain plates, and little knick-knacks. It was set up nicely and was often well-dusted. On holidays or on other occasions my mom had company, we would eat with those dishes. Later, I learned that whatever was in the China cabinet was not just for eating.

One early Saturday morning while it was still dark outside, my mom came home drunk. My sisters and I were in bed. She came into my room screaming and hollering about how the house wasn't clean. "How is that you hussies in the bed when my house ain't clean?" She flipped the light switch on while leaning on the wall because she couldn't stand up straight. I was still trying to wake up, lifting one hand in front of my eyes to block the blinding lights so I could gain my full vision back. In a cracked, yet shaky voice, I said, "Mommy, we did our chores before we went to bed." That was like talking back to my mother. Like most parents, she was very contradicting in her arguments; she wanted an answer but we couldn't talk to tell her the answer. But I gave it a shot and needless to say, it didn't work out for me. My mom grabbed me, dragging me out of my bed and out of my room. I struggled a lot to get away, but she was just too strong; the more I struggled, the more she felt challenged to overpower me. I was crying words like, "Mom," "please," "stop," "sorry," until we got to the top of the steps, as she lifted me by my neck with one hand yelling, "You think you're so smart." I started crying again as my feet dangled off the floor at the top of the steps. I thought, *this is it; she is going to throw me down these wooden stairs, and I'm gonna break my neck and die.* My sisters were in their rooms crying because they knew not to come out or else, they'd be next. "I should kill your smart ass right now," my mom yelled in my face. I was still pleading with her, but my pleas were not good enough. To her, I was proven guilty, and I had to be punished. My mother threw me down the steps. As I rolled and flipped downstairs, my mother followed quickly behind me, yelling, "I'm not done with your ass yet!" I thought she would have been done with me, but she clearly let me know it wasn't over.

I was in a ball crying, waiting for my punishment to end from the judge who I felt like sentenced me to death. My sisters were now at the top of the steps, trying unsuccessfully to cry quietly. My mother called everyone down the stairs. "Get y'all asses down here now!" she said. Everyone started crying hysterically. My mother punched and kicked me in front of my sisters, blow after blow, everywhere on my body: on my head, stomach, and legs, all with a closed fist. When she was done beating on me, I just lied there in the living room, crying in a ball saying, "I'm sorry, Mommy. I didn't mean to talk back to you." Mommy went into the dining room and into her China cabinet. I thought maybe she was done and was going to have a drink out of one of her fancy glasses, but I was wrong again. She came back in the room with about 10 heavy China plates — the big white ones with the gold ring around the edge of the plates, not the little saucers. "You think you're so smart, hunh?" she said as she walked over to me, although I was still on the floor crying. I could have gotten up and ran around the house, but I knew it would only make things worse. I was too scared to even move the wrong way. Mommy walked over to me with those plates held over her head and kicked my legs out of the ball they were in so that I could be lying flat on my back. It was time for me to face the judge. She stood over me, with me between her legs yelling, "I should kill you right now." I held my hands in front of my face, crying, "No, Mommy, don't do this. I'm sorry!" trying to sell my way out of this death scene. She responded, "Put your hands down. You so smart, face me," she yelled. I did as she ordered, putting my arms flat on the floor beside my legs. My mom readjusted her stance above me, taking her feet from between my arms and legs so that her feet were on the outside of my arms, squeezing my arms closer to my legs. She raised the China plates over her head as if she was going to forcefully drop them on my face. *This is it, she is going to kill me,* I thought. All I could hear was my sister yelling, "Mommy, no, Mommy, no," but no one tried to help me or stop her. They knew what was good for them. It was like she was in a battle with herself: a moment of contemplation regarding whether she was making the right decision, and therefore, needed peace and quiet. She yelled, "Shut the fuck up, shut up!" still holding the plates in front of her. She lifted the plates over her head with a loud war cry. I turned my face to the left as if that would help the impact. I closed my eyes and the next thing I knew, there was a sting all over my legs. She dropped the plates behind her head as she was yelling, and the plates fell all over my legs. I had minor cuts and scrapes, but the pain was unbearable. She walked away, saying, "I should have killed yo' ass. Get up and clean this shit up, and I want it spic and span." I jumped up quickly, kneeling and whimpering, trying to fight through the pain and trauma of what just felt like a 30-minute horror scene. My sister Fifi tried to come and help me, but my mother yelled, "Get your ass upstairs, unless you want to be next!" Fifi quickly ran upstairs, without even looking back, and Lyfe ran upstairs, while Sophie scooted her way back up the stairs and went to bed crying. I just started cleaning up glass, acting as if I dropped a few plates by accident because the last thing I wanted to do was make a scene like *I'm really hurt*.

As I cleaned up the debris from the China plates, my legs felt like they were on fire. There was blood running down them, and I walked with a limp. My mom just stood there, watching from the living room as she smoked her cigarette and drank her Colt 45. I was petrified. She watched me as I limped from the living room to the kitchen to get a trash bag, broom, and dust pan. My mom stopped me in the dining room, saying, "Why are you limping?" I thought to myself *She, is fucking crazy. If I wasn't scared, I would slit your fucking throat with a piece of a China plate.* I kept my thoughts to myself because I wasn't sure of the outcome; she may have definitely succeeded at killing me if those actual words came out of my mouth. Instead, I answered, "I fell down the stairs," as I looked down at the floor. My mother said, "Good girl." See, every time she would give me a beating that left a mark or would cause me to limp, I was programmed to say I fell down the stairs. Sometimes, she would switch the story up and tell me to say something different. I had to go to school in two days, so I had to have my story straight if I was still going to be limping. Actually, I limped for about two days, so by the time I got back to school, I was fine. After creating my alibi, I quickly finished my work in the living room. I picked up the big pieces first, and then I swept as many of the small pieces I could into a pile and placed them in the trash bag. After I finished, I put the bag out on the front porch for trash day. My mother came to me, grabbed me by my neck and told me, "If you ever talk back to me again, I will put you 6 ft under. Do you understand me?" I uttered, "Yes, ma'am." She let me go, forcefully pushing me away, yelling "Now go clean yourself up, and get your ass in the bed." Once again, I uttered, "Yes, ma'am," and I went to nurse my own wounds with peroxide and cotton balls and put band aids all over my legs. I wiped the now dried up blood off my legs and feet and then went to bed, thinking of suicide. I honestly thought about different ways I could kill myself and get out of this hellhole I was in, *I could hold my breath until I die, I could cut myself and bleed to death.* The last thought I had about suicide was, *I can't even commit suicide because I'm afraid that mommy will come and kill me again for killing myself.* The fear I had of my mother crippled my whole thought process about everything. Instead of staying up all night thinking of ways to off myself, I just began crying myself to sleep quietly, because God forbid my mother heard my thoughts. Fifi and Sophie whom I shared the room with were still awake, and they both whispered, "We're so sorry." Fifi said, "I'm gonna kill her ass one day." I couldn't respond, so I just cried myself to sleep.

The Prayer

On the lonely two mile walk to school that Monday, (Fifi was suspended by herself this time), I had a talk with God. I wasn't sure if he existed, or if he would answer a small 12-year-old person like me. Going to church wasn't really in my routine, but somehow, I always had the urge to pray or attempt to pray to God. My family were what church goers call "CME" members: people who only show up to church on Christmas, Mother's Day, and Easter. Although I don't remember ever stepping foot in a church building, because I was too young to remember, my mother had pictures that showed otherwise. Maybe God was listening to my prayer, maybe He does know my heart.

After my life flashed before my eyes the other day with the "China Plates" incident, I started to think about my purpose. I prayed to God, *why am I here? Am I just here to be beat on and made fun of? God, please help me; take me away from all of this mess. I love my mom, but I don't think she loves me back. God, help her to love me the way I love her. Help her love all of my sisters so she can stop beating us. It hurts so bad when she beats us. God, please help the kids at school to stop bullying me; I just want to learn. I don't even like to fight; that hurts, too. God, if you are out there, please help my mother, my sisters, and me. Amen.*

The Last Straw

Home and school were like great big arenas; however, they both were their own separate entities. Fifi used school as her own little arena, and Mommy used home as her own little arena. I just simply entered both arenas on a technicality of living. Fifi was the one always getting us into fights at school. It was like as soon as we entered the school doors, the fighter's bell went off in Fifi's head. *Ding, ding.* She was ready to fight. This one time, Fifi and I were walking up the stairs, along with hundreds of other kids, at the first bell. One girl accidentally bumped Fifi as she was walking up the stairs. *Oh God*, I thought to myself; I knew all hell was about to break loose.

Fifi stopped and said, "Bitch say excuse me next time, or that's gone be yo' ass!"

"It was an accident; there are a lot of us trying to fit up this one stairwell, calm down. Besides, I don't feel like dealing with Mommy when we get home," I said, trying to get Fifi to calm down.

Fifi continued to carry on, "No, no, cause, I know that bitch saw me; she could have waited or moved over a little bit!" The other girl was walking ahead when she heard Fifi carrying on. "I don't know who the fuck you think ya talking to, bitch. I didn't even know I bumped you," the other girl said. *See, she didn't mean to do it,* I thought, but then things just got out of control. Fifi ran up the next few steps onto the last landing post before reaching the doors and grabbed the girl by her hair and just started swinging on her. I ran up after her trying to get Fifi off of the girl when another girl jumped in and started swinging on me. How quickly events changed from me trying to stop a fight to me getting into a fight, so I defended myself and started fighting this girl. The crowd was loud and moved us out of the stairwell through the double doors and into the hallway on the second floor. We were fighting for a good two minutes before the NTA (non-teaching assistant) Ms. Jenkins broke up the crowd and our fight. Ms. Jenkins was mean, and I could tell she didn't like me or Fifi. She would always hound us every time we walked by her in the hallway. We could be walking in the hallway alone late for class, and she'd fuss at us; or, we could be walking with others and she'd still choose to fuss at us. This fight was the last straw; she was tired of us. "You two at it again! That's it, you're getting suspended," Ms. Jenkins said as she grabbed both of us by our arms as tight as she could. Fifi and I were trying to get out of her firm grip, but Ms. Jenkins was not letting up.

As we were forcefully and painfully escorted to the principal's office, I said to Fifi, "See, it's all your fault. Now we gonna get suspended and get our asses beat when we get home."

Fifi responded, "Shut up, we were gonna get our asses beat anyway when we got home."

I didn't respond, but I knew she was telling the truth. She was right; we didn't have to do anything particularly wrong to get a beating. All we had to do was wake up in the morning, and we would win a guaranteed good ole-fashioned butt whooping. In fact, there was a time in my life where Fifi and I got a beating every day for no reason, other than because my mother was drunk. It became a norm, like taking medicine for a chronic illness. Anyway, when we reached the principal's office,

Principal Luck looked at us and said, "Three days, don't come back without your mother." We didn't get a chance to explain anything, not that we had an explanation that would get us out of the suspension, but she was just tired of seeing our faces in her office. The school day was just beginning, and we were already suspended. We had gone to the In-School Suspension Room for the rest of the day with other students who were in trouble. I had to go through the rest of the school day dreading what was going to happen when we got home. *Was my mother going to choke me, throw me down some stairs, give me a regular beating, or worse?* I gave myself a headache thinking about it.

    The last bell rang, the school day ended, and my heart started pounding out of my chest. *God, please help us, and don't let it be too bad,* I prayed to myself. I knew I was about to step into the home arena, a scarier, and somewhat deadly arena. I was not ready to face the consequences that lay ahead. Fifi and I took the long way home. Our walk was already two miles, so we really didn't need to take any longcuts, but we did. Although it never worked, normally on the way home from a troubled day, we would try to make up some bogus lie or story of what happened to make it sound better and avoid getting a beating. This day was different: The walk home was silent, with Fifi and I not saying a word. I think we both were preparing ourselves for what was to come. I'm pretty sure Fifi was thinking about stuff; I know I was at some point, but then I had no thoughts at all. It was like my brain was empty. We finally reached home, opened the front door to the house, walked in, and there was my mother sitting on the couch with an extension cord in her hand. I started to cry immediately, while Fifi, on the other hand, had a blank look on her face, a face my mother hated. Mommy said that Fifi's blank look makes her feel like she doesn't care, or that she isn't afraid of my mother. Whenever my mother saw that face, she felt challenged. It was like she had to beat us harder or longer so that she could be sure we were afraid. See, normally my mother was the type of parent who asked you whether you wanted to get a beating or go on punishment. No matter what we said, she always did both. This particular day, she didn't even give us a choice; she just did both. "Strip, both of you," my mother said as soon as we got through the door. I was crying while taking off my clothes, but Fifi was taking off her clothes with that blank stare on her face. Sometimes I wanted to beat the shit out of Fifi just to wipe that blank stare off her face. My mother walked toward us with her brown 12-inch extension cord. She held onto both ends of the cord, with the plug part and socket part in one hand, as the loop was left hanging. As we were still taking off our clothes, my mom started yelling at us, "You dumb bitches always getting yourselves in trouble. Y'all don't have nothin' else better to do than to fight. I send you to school to learn, and I have to keep getting these phone calls home, and now y'all got to stay home for three days. Oh, hell NO!" As we stood there, butt naked listening to my mother yell and come toward us, I just closed my eyes waiting for it to be over. My mother started whipping us all over our bodies. Whip after whip was painful, leaving welts on our bare skin. Fifi and I were falling all over each other, and my mother was kicking and hitting us with the extension cord. No matter how tough Fifi or her blank stare was, no one could stand my mother's whipping without crying, screaming, and hollering. The both of us were crying and rolling all around the floor waiting for the beating to stop. After what seemed to be eternity, a few minutes later, the beating stopped. Although it was over, Fifi and I were still crying in so much pain with all the swelling and bruising. You'd be surprised at the marks an extension cord can leave on scrawny little 11 and 12-year-old girls. My mom didn't want to hear us crying, so she yelled, "Stop all that damn noise before I give you something else to cry for." She ordered us to clean up the house right away. "Get the fuck out of my face and clean this house; I want this house spic and span when I come back!" my mother yelled. Fifi and I jumped up, put our clothes on, and got right to cleaning as ordered. My mother left the house and did not return until the next afternoon, per usual. By this time, my sisters Lyfe and Sophie were just getting home from school. Lyfe was in charge of us whenever my mother left, and she was ordered not to feed us until the house was "spic and span," as my mother said with tight lips. Although we cleaned it the best we could, Lyfe the Judge did not think it was good enough. Sometimes Lyfe enjoyed seeing

Fifi and me in pain and in trouble. As previously mentioned, Lyfe didn't get many beatings because she had sickle cell. I guess my mother felt it would be wrong to beat a sickly child, even though Lyfe was worse than Fifi and me. Needless to say, Fifi and I did not eat that night.

The next morning, I woke everyone up for school and got everyone ready for school. I made sure everyone was washed and ready to go to school. Lyfe left the house to go to pretend school (she cut school every day), Sophie got picked up by her school bus, and I had walked my two nieces and nephew to their daycare. When I came back home, Fifi and I sat down to relax. The house was cleaned; there was nothing else to do because we were on punishment. We couldn't watch TV, listen to music, or do anything fun (as if we did that kind of stuff on a regular day). We just sat around. That afternoon before everyone got home from school, my mother walked in the house after being out all night. Fifi and I were sitting in the living room on the couch. As soon as we heard my mother's keys in the door, we sat straight up on the couch like we were waiting patiently for her to tell us what to do next.

She was as drunk as a skunk. I could tell by the way she stammered through the door and stood at the doorway staring at us.

"Oh, so y'all don't have anything else to do, huh?" my mother said in a sluggish voice.

Fifi answered, "We cleaned the whole house like you said, Mommy."

I sat silently waiting for the conversation to end, when my mother yelled, "You got all the answers, hunh bitch? I'mma show you who smarter."

Now I thought that because my mom was drunk that this would be a short and not so hurtful beating, but I was wrong. Boy, was I wrong!

My mother walked over to Fifi, grabbed her by her hair, yanked her off the couch and started dragging her out of the living room and up the stairs. Fifi placed her hand on my mother's hand that had her hair, trying to get out of her grip. I was crying because I didn't know if I was next and also because I hated seeing Fifi get a beating and my mom act this way. My mother always went overboard with Fifi as if she hated her. They struggled up the stairs, as my mother still had her hair and Fifi tried to grab the banister. "You a smart-ass bitch, hunh? We'll see," my mother said. Fifi was kicking, screaming, and crying, but my mother just kept going. They got to the top of the last step, which was the 14th step, and my mother began to beat Fifi with her bare hand, punching her, kicking her, and knocking her all around the narrow hallway. The hallway was very narrow, about 15 inches wide and 10 ft long. My mother beat Fifi from wall to wall, from the stairs to the back room. I followed behind them, scared for Fifi's life. I didn't understand the movement during a beating; this was new to me. They finally made it to the back room, and my mother was still beating on Fifi. The back room was a nice sized room. At the right of the entrance was a set of bunk beds where Fifi and I slept, and to the left was another set of bunk beds where Lyfe and Sophie slept. There was about 5 ft of space between the sets of bunk beds. Opposite of the door was a low window in the middle of the wall. My mother beat Fifi until she pinned her up against the window. I felt so helpless; I wanted to call the cops, but I was scared to do that.

I wanted to attack my mother, but I was afraid to do that, too. So many thoughts ran through my mind on how I could kill my mother in this instance to stop all of this. *I could get a two-by-four stick and beat her upside the head with it, or I could just go downstairs and get a knife and stab her dead,* I thought. Instead of acting on any of those thoughts, I was just stuck crying hopelessly, wishing that it would be over.

My mother did not let up; she continued beating and choking Fifi, yelling, "I will kill you. I will kill you, bitch." She continuously struck her until she turned Fifi around, grabbed her by her hair, and then knocked her head against the window.

Fifi was crying, screaming, and yelling, "Help me, stop Mommy."

I was crying and yelling, "Mommy, stop! Please stop, Mommy", but my mother kept on knocking Fifi's head against the window.

Fifi used her hands to block her face from hitting the window a few times, but my mother got angrier. She took Fifi's hands and held them behind her back with one hand, and with the other hand, was still grabbing Fifi's hair, knocking her head up against the window. Next thing you know, the last blow to the window had Fifi's head hanging out the window. Fifi's head went through the glass and through the window screen. Glass shattered, and blood splat everywhere. Suddenly, my mother let go of Fifi, Fifi's head still hanging out of the three-story window with blood dripping from her head and face. My mother backed away from Fifi like she was scared of something or like she had suddenly seen a ghost. I ran past my mother and grabbed Fifi helping her out of the window, holding her in my arms crying, saying, "I'm sorry, sister. I'm so sorry, sister." My mother sprang into action and separated us from each other, grabbing Fifi and rushing down the hallway and into the bathroom to rinse her face off in a small bathroom sink. Fifi was screaming and crying as my mother was washing her face. I was yelling, "Mommy, she needs to go to the hospital. There is too much blood." I couldn't see much of Fifi's face just then; I just saw blood all over the place. When my mother stopped rinsing Fifi's face with water, there was still blood dripping everywhere. There was a big gash at the top of her head where her hair line was. It was about 3 to 5 inches long, just pink meat hanging out of her head with blood oozing out of her gash. There were other small shards of glass still stuck in Fifi's face, and she had a busted nose and mouth. It was all so horrifying to see. I called 911 immediately after I saw that. I didn't care what my mother had to say. As the line first rang, I prayed to God, *please help my sister.*

"Hello, what's your emergency?" the operator said.

"Please help, my sister is hurt. There is blood coming out of her head; there is blood everywhere," I cried.

The operator asked the usual questions like, "Where do you live?" and "How old are you?" and I answered them correctly.

"Are you in danger?" the operator asked.

I looked at my mom, and she shook her head no to me with this crazy look on her face, as if I would be next if I told the truth.

"Um, u-h no, no, ma'am, my sister hurt herself," I cried, lying through my teeth.

They asked a few other questions, and the ambulance and police came right away. My mother and I rode in the car behind the ambulance. I could tell my mother was afraid of something.

She kept telling me, "You better keep your damn mouth shut. Don't you tell what happens in this house, you hear me?"

I cried, stuttering, "Yes, ma'am."

"You keep your mouth shut or you are going to be next, you hear me?" she said.

I just cried and cried until we reached the hospital. There were so many evil thoughts going through my head; I wanted to take over the wheel and kill us both. I just wanted my mother to be dead at that moment. There was no holding this secret; it was too big of a secret, but out of fear, I did as I was told.

When my mother and I arrived at the hospital, Fifi was being rolled out on a stretcher from the ambulance truck into the hospital. We caught up with the two gentlemen who were rolling Fifi into the emergency entrance of Children's Hospital of Philadelphia. As they approached the automatic doors, there were a few doctors and a few nurses already there waiting to receive Fifi.

"Are you the mother?" one doctor asked, looking at my

mother. "Yes, I am," my mother replied with a shaky voice. The EMT workers said a lot of medical terms to the nurses and doctors as they grabbed Fifi's gurney. The only term I was familiar with was "surgery." I cried to Fifi: "I love you. I'm sorry," as the doctors rolled her through the big gray double doors that only hospital employees were able to enter. My mother and I were stopped at those double doors by the nurses. "Ma'am you can't come back here. We have to operate on her now. Please wait in the waiting area, and someone will be out to notify you about your daughter," one nurse said to my mother with a sense of demand and urgency in her voice. I was so afraid for my sister. I was shaking, and Fifi's blood was all over my hands and my shirt. It was very tragic and traumatizing. My mother and I just went to sit down in the waiting area as we were ordered; we sat in silence.

A few minutes after Fifi was taken back for surgery, another doctor came out to ask my mother what happened. I quickly glanced up at the doctor with a frightened look, not knowing what my mother would say. Remembering the conversation in the car ride over, "Don't say a word," I knew I wasn't allowed to speak.

"Ma'am, I just have a few questions for you concerning your daughter," the doctor said. "How old is your daughter?" My mother muttered, "Uh, she is uh, uh 11 years old."

"Can you tell me what happened to Phoenix?" the doctor asked.

"Uh, she was running in the hallway at the top of the steps and fell down the steps," my mother answered.

I just put my head down in my lap, covering my face with my hands. I was sighing, trying not to burst into uncontrollable tears.

"Okay, I see. It looks like she was running pretty fast because the injuries and bruises she has is severe. She has a fractured skull that is going to need a metal plate in her head to help it heal and a few stitches, but she will be okay. The surgery should take a few hours, but as soon as she is out of surgery, you will be able to go in and see your daughter." *That's it*, I thought. *Just like that, once again, my mom was going to get away with her abusive ways.*

Fifi was out of surgery and in the recovering room

when we were called back to see her. The doctors had already spoken to Fifi before my mom and I came into the room. They asked her questions about if she remembered what happened to her. Fifi lied and told the doctor she was playing outside and ran into a pole. She gave the wrong story, which drew attention to my mother. My mom forgot to tell Fifi the story before going to the hospital. She said it a few times to me, but not to Fifi. So, the doctor asked Fifi in front of my mother what happened, and she said the same thing: She was playing outside and ran into a pole. At this point, a few officers came into the hospital room to take information. Fifi cried out saying, "I was playing outside and ran into a pole," as she looked down at her feet, avoiding contact from my mother. My mom just stared at us, not saying a word. She was staring at the both of us to make sure we didn't betray her trust. After the last lie, Fifi was cleared to go home within a few days.

The Great Separation

About a few months later — although I remember it like it was yesterday, a replay I wish would be expunged from my mind — came the day of the great separation (even though it didn't feel so great). Lyfe, Fifi, Sophie, my two nieces, my nephew, and I were in the house sitting around watching TV. There was a knock at the door one day after school, and my mother wasn't home. No one moved to open the door because if my mom found out that we opened the door for anyone, that was going to be our backsides. She always said, "Don't open this door for nobody, you understand me? Don't even open the door for me because I have a key to get in my own house." The knock grew stronger, with a voice saying, "Girls, open the door. It's Ms. Casey from DHS."

I yelled "We can't open the door; our mommy said not to answer the door for anyone when she is not home."

Ms. Casey yelled back, "Your mother cannot hurt you; we have your mother. We need you to open the door."

Fifi, *being one of the rebels in the house,* opened the

door. I was as scared as ever thinking of my mother's wrath, but Fifi opened the door. Ms. Casey rushed through the doors, giving everyone a black plastic bag. At the time, there were seven of us living with my mom: my three sisters, two nieces, my nephew, and me. We were all given one bag to collect as much as we could. "Hurry! Gather whatever you have that can fit in this bag. We are here to take you to a new home so that you all can be safe," Ms. Casey said. Sophie and I began to cry, and Sophie cried hysterically. She was the least likely to get beat by my mother because she was in a wheelchair so I could understand her crying, not wanting to leave our mom. It's funny, though, because I got a lot of good beatings, but I still cried because I loved my mother. Although I loved her, I was tired of being beaten every day. So many thoughts went through my mind as I began to pack my things: *Where will we go? I always wanted to run away from home but was always so scared that Mommy would find me and the beating would just be worse. If we leave now, Mommy will find us and punish us all.* I had a really hard time grasping what was happening, I grabbed my green comfort sheet I kept after Isabella ran away, crying trying to calm myself down. It was then that I started keeping the sheet close to me, rubbing it against my nose and face, pinching and squeezing it for comfort. Still to this day, my sheet calms me down when I'm angry, sad, mad, sleepy or scared. Today, I was very anxious and needed my sheet. No one asked any questions; everyone just started packing. I was kind of confused as to why all of a sudden, we were getting taken away from my mother. After all we had gone through, why now? It turned out that Lyfe was at school broadcasting what happened to Fifi and the whole "head out the window incident." As word got around, word fell on the ears of the principal and school counselor. Within the next month after the incident, my mother was under investigation for Fifi's case, and she was found guilty. That is why Ms. Casey showed up to take us away for good. It wasn't just Ms. Casey; there were three other people helping us put different clothing items in the bags and a few police officers. They asked us questions like, "Can you show me what your mother used to hit you with?" We pulled out shoes, two-by-fours, wooden planks, broom and mop sticks, extension cords,

China plates, and glasses. Eventually, they were so disturbed by all the items we were picking up, they were like, "Okay, that's enough." One lady asked us to show our bodies for bruises. She took pictures of our skinny, bruised bodies (well, Fifi's and my bruised bodies). Fifi had fresh bruises on her, which is what made them take us away in the first place. Fifi had been beaten less than a month ago before being hospitalized by my mother. She had a scar from the stitches on her head from the metal plate the doctors put in her head. While we were being taken away, my mother was found wherever she was, and taken into custody by police officers. My mother served a few months in jail for the incident. After they finished checking our bodies, Ms. Casey rushed us out the door with our black plastic bags. *It's all our fault,* I thought. *We didn't listen, and we made Mommy hurt us the way she did.*

Thoughts continued to flood my mind, even the feeling of relief to know we would be somewhere safe. I was so confused and hurt by all the emotions I was feeling. As we left the house, everyone on the block was outside as if they knew what was happening. Our neighbors all came up to hug and console us, telling us to be strong and that it's okay. All of that made me cry and realize how much danger we were actually in living with my mother. When you're so deep in a situation and it becomes the norm, you start to actually believe that it's normal. Getting the daylights beat out of me had definitely become my normal. I thought it was love; I thought that maybe that's what mothers did to their children. I also thought that maybe it wasn't regular love, but M*ommy's love*. Ms. Casey broke up the farewells and goodbyes by letting everyone know that we had to go and that we would be well-taken care of from here. We boarded the white 15-passenger DHS van. I remember sitting all the way in the back with my face toward the back window, waving and now hysterically crying as the van drove off. I could see the kids on the block running down the street after the big white van. So many overwhelming feelings came upon me. Despite not getting along with many people on the block, it was nice to see they actually cared about us and once again they showed up for us, and didn't want us to leave. I grabbed my green sheet, rubbing it all over my face and pinching it, and continued crying. All I could do was think about the good (the very few good) and fun times I had with my mom and getting into trouble on the block. It was all over, and we'd probably never return again. During the ride, Ms. Casey explained that there were too many of us and that we would have to live in separate homes. There were seven of us that needed to be placed, but no one had enough space for us all. The best they could do was to keep us coupled. Hearing this made everyone upset. Even Lyfe snapped, "Oh, hell no. We are all going together or we're not going nowhere," as if she had a say so. I just cried and cried; *now I have to be separated from my sisters and my nieces and nephew, I thought. Where would I go? Who would I be coupled with? Will we all get the chance to meet up again?* So many thoughts. It turned out that we were able to find one lady named Ms. Mae who took four of us in her home. She took my three sisters — Fifi, Sophie, and Lyfe — and me into her home. My niece and nephew went to one home, and my other niece went to a home by herself. It was the hardest thing to see, hear, and experience. It broke my heart to see my nieces and nephew cry the way they cried. I am the one who took care of all of us. I babysat my nieces and nephews, taught my sisters how to read, and so much more. Now I have to just let them go and try to remember the good times. My life just unraveled, and I couldn't hide my emotions; it was simply too much to handle. We all got dropped off at our separate locations, wondering if we'd ever meet up again.

www.ingramcontent.com/pod-product-compliance
Lightning Source LLC
Chambersburg PA
CBHW050324010526
44119CB00003B/102